Critical Analysis of Jawaharlal Nehru's Financial Planning Policy on National Economy

Critical Analysis of Jawaharlal Nehru's Financial Planning Policy on National Economy

Ashok M Gadkari

GYAN

Published, 2021

Published by

Gyan Publishing House
5, Ansari Road
Daryaganj, New Delhi-110002
Phone: 011-47034999, 9811692060
www.gyanbooks.com
E-mail: books@gyanbooks.com

Printed at: Gyan Press, Delhi.

Cataloging in Publication Data—DK
Courtesy: D.K. Agencies (P) Ltd. <docinfo@dkagencies.com>

Gadkari, Ashok M., 1943- **author.**
Critical analysis of Jawaharlal Nehru's financial planning policy on national economy / Ashok M Gadkari.
pages cm
Includes index.
ISBN 9788121220446

1. India—Economic policy—1947- 2. Nehru, Jawaharlal, 1889-1964. I. Title.

LCC HC435.2.G33 2021 | DDC 338.954009045 23

Contents

Foreword

I am very proud that the author has completed third book on Economics during the last two years. The Author has selected the topic of how much progress India has made after Independence in the field of agriculture, capital goods, public sector, heavy industries under Government of India as well as the Infrastructure and transport performance success in five years plans and performance in defence sector. Critical observations of the Author are accurate and the Author has been rightly impressed by the tremendous successful implementation of plan performance. The book is worth readable. Author knowledge of various sectors is much appreciated.

Mr. Manohar Kanchan

Observations of the Author on Indian Economy are well appreciated. The book shows the progress made by the Govt. of India in various large sector to make India self-sufficient in agriculture, industrial production especially in capital goods heavy industries. Defence was last priority and we did not make good preparation in defence to counter-attack the Chinese aggression in 1961. Thereafter we made good progress in defence and infrastructure to progress our economy tremendously. Difficulties experienced during planning period were successfully overcome. I am also very much impressed like Author on the economic policies adopted by Prime Minister Jawahar Nehru after independence.

Mr. Narayan Nerurkar

Critical Analysis of Jawaharlal Nehru's Financial Planning Policy on National Economy

Introduction

British rule in India was for about 150 years from 1800-1947 when India got independent from British rule on midnight of August 1947. During the British rule, India was ruined economically by the Britishers. Prior to British, Mughal Empire ruled the country. That time, Indian economy was prosperous. Agriculture was prime occupation and lands were cultivated for foodgrains and cotton production. There were handlooms on which the cotton was converted into cloth and was sold to the Indians and foreign market. Silk was particularly in demand in European countries. Foodgrains were surplus and were exported.

After British came to rule India, the land which was used for cultivation of the foodgrains was used for production of cotton. There was shortage of foodgrains and people were starving for food and many deaths occurred on account of famine. In destruction of epidemics, Britishers destroyed the houses of the families resulting in death of thousands/lakhs.

Cotton was produced from India and was transported to England to manufacture cloth in the factories in UK set up under industrial revolution. Cloth manufactured was sent to India for sale where there was large market for sale. Handlooms in India were totally destructed and they were banned to sell cloth manufactured by looms in India. Britishers were so cunning that they forced the loom owners to increase wages of their workers substantially so that cost of Indian cloth was higher than sale price of cloth brought from UK and thus there was no market for sale of Indian cloth. Thus, Handloom trade in India was completely ruined by cruel Britishers.

India was very poor when Britishers left the country on 15th August 1947. Agriculture and foodgrains production were ruined,

Population was starving, there was serious poverty in India and the country was on the verge of collapse.

There was scarcity of food and therefore grocer shops were given government licences to act as the Rationing shops to distribute food to the people having rationing cards. Under PL 480 Scheme, red wheats were used to be brought from USA which were distributed by the rationing shops to the people. I remember that sometimes, Delhi rice equivalent to present Basmati rice was distributed in the rationing shops and public used to stand in big queue to get Delhi rice as it was in great demand. But quantity of food was very small on the ration cards. There was shortage of kerosene which was available on the ration shop. Prices of these commodities were fixed by the government and people had to buy at this price from the ration shops. The price of the government was low compared to the price of such goods available in the black market and since the income of the people was low, only middle class and rich people used to buy such goods like kerosene in the black market.

There was necessity to cultivate land for agriculture with modern and improved methods like use of improve cultivation by tractors, improved seeds, improved fertilisers and irrigation projects.

There was urgent need to take initiative to change and improve these poor economic conditions of India. Agriculture needs to be given priority to increase foodgrains substantially to enable each person to get adequate food and make self-sufficient in agriculture. This required the productivity of agriculture to be improved with better cultivation method, improved fertilisers, to use of tractors. In short, modern technology needs to be used to increase productivity of agriculture and production of foodgrains to make nation self-sufficient. In respect of other fields, the improved quality products needs to be produced.

There were two alternatives available to India to develop Indian economy in other fields than agriculture improvement such as oil and natural gas, national thermal power, steel, heavy electricals and construction of roads, railways, ships and aero planes. There was highest unemployment in India and that serious issue needs to be addressed on priority basis. Defence needs to be improved but there were so many priorities that defence expenditure which is known to be unproductive was given the last priority. There were no sufficient funds for defence improvement.

For the industrial development, there were two alternatives in India. Mahatma Gandhi and his supporters were of the opinion that in rural areas, small scale industries should be set up to give additional/ supplemental source of income to rural population. This will also give employment to the urban population and there will be mass production of various goods. This was similar to the Japanese model. Here the mass production was available but the quality of the goods will be inferior to the goods manufactured in factories with highest developed machinery based on advanced technology. In modern competitive world, quality of goods is most preferred. For international trade, this factor needs to be taken into account while selecting the alternatives.

Mr. Jawaharlal Nehru was the 1st famous prime minister of India from Independence on 15th August 1947 to 27th May 1964 till his death. His birthday is on 14th November 1989 which is known as Children day as he used to like the children most. He was known as "Cha Cha Nehru". In one of the National Congress Conferences, he advocated strongly the model of socio-economic planning policy for the prosperity of the Indian economy as implemented by USSR and China. In fact, he was very much impressed of this five year plan policy adopted by these countries. He was of the opinion that large scale Public Sector Capital goods like setting up railways, road and air transportation, steel, oil and natural gas, heavy electricals, coal and petroleum companies should be established exclusively under the ownership and control of the Government of India. Their capital should be raised entirely by Government of India and cost of import of modern advanced technology machinery with foreign technicians to train our officials and labours to operate these machine with optimum utilisation should be paid by raising external debts on sovereign account and the repayment of loan should be entire responsibility of the Indian Government. These productive advanced machinery should be set up in such a way that in process of production, we should get maximum/optimum production. Plan should be made to ascertain the break-even period to repay the loans and period of commencing profitable production. Repayment or servicing loan upto the profitable stage may result deficit financing and may result in loan rescheduling and piling of loan amount of the Government of India. But this way, the production of electricity, coal, petrol, natural gas, steel, primary products and infrastructure such as railways, roads and air will tremendously increase and will make the nation more prosperous. The accurate planning and critical appraisal of the plan implementation at each stage was required. These large scale industries will give employment to large unemployed young skilled and unskilled workers and will reduce the unemployment problem substantially. Agricultural cultivation with modern immunities such as improved fertilizers, tractors, improved seeds and better irrigation facilities will improve the Indian economy and will give employment to rural population in a big way.

First Five Year Plan commenced in 1951-56 and there the priority was given to agriculture, irrigation, improved cultivation and improved seeds. Total outlay of the plan was ₹ 2060 crores out of which 40% was for agriculture and 15% for heavy industries. Rest was for infrastructure development.

While inaugurating Atal Tunnel which opens a shorter all weather route underneath the Rohtang Pass linking Manali to Leh in a record period of 8 years, Honourable Prime Minister Mr. Narendra Modi said that in Congress rule, this Tunnel and other defence preparation were neglected. No doubt, this will cut the travel time from Manali to Leh by 4-5 times and is very appreciable and commendable work. But remark made by honorable Prime Minister on Congress rule on defence is not true.

As will be seen above, after independence, there were so much priorities for agriculture, industrialisation and unemployment that defence was last priority as there was no funds for defence sector. Indian population had very small income with each family and the saving capacity of each family was negligible and no small investment under the Public Debt can be raised in large amount even with high rate of interest. Therefore, the defence was not given priority and Jawaharlal Nehru preached Panch Sheel and disarmament policy to the world but cunning China took this advantage and attacked India and defeated it by annexing Tibet as part of China. Thereafter Congress made progress in acquiring military equipments from many countries including USSR and defeated Pakistan in 1965 and 1971 wars. Narendra Modi should not forget that its government is able to give priorities to Defence today on account of tremendous economic progress by introducing Five Year Plans with successful implementation by Honorable Jawaharlal Nehru and his successors. I am very much impressed by the growth of heavy industries made by five year plan policy by Jawaharlal Nehru.

The First Five Year Plan was launched in 1951. It had a great role of Indian development after Independence. It strongly supported the agriculture production and then Industrialisation of the country. The Second Plan commenced from 1957 which gave the priority to industrialisation. Import of capital goods machinery was made in that period. But since Indian economy has scarce foreign exchange reserves, this resulted in deficit financing and in 1957, this resulted in foreign exchange crisis. Classical economist Mr. B.R. Shenoy criticised Second Plan as calling for trouble. Crisis in 1957 confirmed his criticism.

In the first five year plan, utmost priority was given for agriculture production. Size of the Plan was ₹ 2069 crores originally which was revised to ₹ 2378 crores. Five Year Plan was based on Harrod-Domar model with few modifications. Total plan expenditure was allocated to seven broad areas such as Irrigation and Energy 27.2%, agriculture and community development 17.4%, transport and communication 24%, industries 8.4%, Social services 16.6%, rehabilitation of landless farmers 4.1% and other sectors and services 2.5%.

Target rate was 2.1% but actual growth was 3.6% on account of good monsoon and there were relatively high crop yield. Per capita income increased and Net Domestic Product went up by 3.6%. Many Irrigation Projects were initiated during this period, including Bakra-Nangal, Hirakud, Mettur, Damodar Valley dams. This reduced the water shortage and generated huge amount of electricity to make India self-sufficient in electricity demand. WHO with Indian Government addressed children health and reduced infant mortality, indirectly contributing to population growth.

At the end of the Plan in 1956, five Indian Institutions of Technology were started as major technical institutions with the help of USSR. University Grant Commission was also set up to take care of funding and take measures to strengthen high education in the country. Contracts were signed to start five steel plants which came into existence in the middle of the Second Five Year Plan. Plan was quasi successful for the government.

In Second Five Year Plan (1957-61), Economic development model was developed by the statistician Prasanta Chandra Mahalanobis in 1953.

Plan attempted to determine the optimal allocations of the investment between the productive sectors and to maximize long-term economic growth. It used the prevalent state-of-art techniques of operation research and optimisation as well as the novel application of statistic model at the Indian Statistical Institute.

Hydroelectric Power Project and five steel plants at Bhilai, Durgapur, and Rourkela were established with the help of Russia, Britain and West Germany. Coal production was increased. More railway lines were added in the north-east.

Tata Institute of Fundamental Research and Atomic Energy Commission of India were established in 1957. Talent search and scholarship programmes began to find talented young students to train for work in nuclear power.

Total amount allocated to the plan was ₹ 4800 crores. The amount was allocated among power and irrigation, social services, communication, transport and miscellaneous. The Second Plan was a period of rising prices. Country faced foreign exchange crisis. The rapid growth in population slowed down the growth in the capital income. Target was 4.5%, Actual achieved was 4.27%. Good compliance.

Chapter - 1

Information on Five Year Plans

Introduction

When India got independence from Britishers in 1947, economy was completely on the verge of destruction. It was necessary to bring the economy on the track and ensure the fastest financial progress be achieved. There were various alternatives to be used to achieve these goals. There was capitalised method of USA to achieve this goal. But Indian Prime Minister Jawaharlal Nehru was very much impressed by the Five Year Plans for such rapid economic growth. Russia's Five Year Planning Policy was adopted in India.

If Five year plans are to be adopted, Planning Commission with Chairman, Vice-Chairman and members of the Planning Commission are required to be appointed. Nehru was the Chairman of the First Planning Commission with statistician Mahalanobis and RBI Governor Mr. C. D. Deshmukh as members of the planning commission. They all discussed and decided the priorities of the country. These priorities were the growth of Agriculture and Rapid Industrial Progress. First Five Year Plan was given priority to agriculture and plan size was Rs. 2392 crores. 40% of these were allocated to irrigation project and improvement of fertilisers. In 1951, agriculture production was very short of meeting needs of the Indian population and there was vast unemployment. 70% of the population used to live in villages with agriculture as their main occupation. Their income was small and they needed supporting job to improve their income.

For Five Year Plan, priorities need to be identified and finalised. In order to improve agriculture, it was necessary to find out the means of improving it. Uncertain monsoon was the first critical issue. There were famines at times and there were floods due to heavy rains. In both these cases, foodgrains production used to be substantially reduced and foodgrains were required to be imported to feed the large Indian population. Farmers' debts were required to be waived with large amount of ₹ 50,000 crores which happened to be routine exercise almost every year. Crop insurance was also not available. Huge amount of funds need to be spent on irrigation and construction of dams, electricity should be provided to the farmers at concessional rates, tractors are to be provided at concessional prices, improved fertilisers need to be distributed on time. In First Five Year plan, however, the monsoon was good and therefore the country could achieve the growth of 5% during the first five year plan 1951-56.

For designing five year plan, the priorities need to be identified and the steps to be taken to achieve the priorities. For example, in agriculture, improved modern methods need to be identified to increase the foodgrains production. Then the funds needed to be assessed and provided. There should be close eye on the implementation of the target to ensure that the targets and priorities are achieved on time. If there are difficulties, these need to be addressed properly and remedies applied to avoid the delay. Large scale modern capital machinery requires huge foreign exchange funds which need to be raised on time with proper schedule of repayment arrangement from IMF or World Bank. Proper attention needs to be made all the times for successful implementation of the priorities on time.

Economic planning

Key economic decisions are made or influenced by central governments. It contrasts with the laissez-faire approach that, in its purest form, eschews any attempt to guide the economy, relying instead on market forces to determine the speed, direction, and nature of economic evolution.

By the late 1960s the majority of the world's countries conducted their economic affairs within the framework of a national economic plan. But in the 1980s the theory and practice of economic planning went through a crisis. In the developed market economies the rate of economic growth slowed from the very high levels reached in the 1960s and '70s, and unemployment rose significantly. At the same time, public confidence in the ability of governments to influence for the better the performance of the economy diminished. As a result, the popularity of national economic plans waned and the scope left to the free play of market forces widened. In developing countries, forms of economic planning practiced earlier yielded disappointing results characterised by the growth of heavy state bureaucracies and inefficient public enterprises. In these countries also, although the role of the state remained preponderant, market forces were increasingly relied upon to improve economic performance. In the Soviet Union and its satellites, the backward state of the economy and widespread examples of waste and inefficiency led to attempts to introduce more market solutions into the process of economic planning. These attempts proved largely unsuccessful, however, and the inherent rigidity of the Soviet economic model proved an important factor in the collapse of communism in Eastern Europe and the Soviet Union itself, beginning in 1989.

The Nature of Economic Planning

Historically, the idea of central economic planning was associated with the criticism of capitalism as a system of anarchy and greed. Marxist critics did not give much thought to how the economy would be run after capitalism had been abolished; most of them professed to see no difficulty in organising the society that would follow. When in 1917 the new Soviet government found itself the owner of all the means of production, it had no blueprint as to what to do next. The evolution of central economic planning in the Soviet Union was largely a pragmatic affair; methods were tried and discarded, and new ones were introduced. The decision in 1927 to undertake rapid and large-scale industrialisation required the centralising of control, since only the government could undertake the task of marshaling the productive resources of the country to achieve its ambitious aims.

In Western Europe, economic planning is adapted to a diversified economic structure, a dynamic class of business managers, and a long tradition of political and economic liberty. Consequently, although planning implies an extension of the economic responsibilities and activities of the state, the mainspring of economic growth remains the private sector. Only rarely does the state intervene directly in the affairs of individual firms. Economic planning remains indirect and takes the form of collaboration between the public and the private sectors. Producers and consumers are free to adapt their activities to changes in market conditions and relative prices. In the 1980s there was a general trend for governments to sell state-owned enterprises to the public and to reduce the extent of public regulation of particular sectors, such as air transport.

Communist methods of planning after the mid-1950s entered a state of flux, and the highly centralised administrative type of planning inherited after World War II from the Soviet Union by all the newly established communist states underwent considerable modifications. In Yugoslavia planners followed policies very different from those of the Soviet model, and differences also emerged in the practice of other eastern European countries. In the Soviet Union itself, a debate concerning the most appropriate means for implementing plans went on for some years, but, despite numerous efforts on the part of the government to reorganise the machinery of planning, the fundamental drawbacks of central economic planning were never overcome. The Soviet Union's attempts in the late 1980s to reform its planning machinery had the unintended effect of bringing down the whole structure of central economic planning, and with it the Soviet government itself. By the early 1990s the post-communist governments of the Eastern Europe and of the states of the former Soviet Union had begun making a painful transition to the diversified economic structure typical of the economies of Western Europe.

In the meantime, the knowledge of the Soviet-bloc countries' long-standing difficulties had given rise in many developing countries to a repugnance to Soviet planning methods, while the methods used in the developed noncommunist countries were felt to be not directly applicable, either. There was consequently no settled planning doctrine in the developing countries, and the approach of governments remained empirical. In practice, this meant that the state played a major role in setting up new industries and in modernising agriculture, particularly in countries of recent independence. The state budget was a major source of savings, supplemented frequently by the local currency counterpart of foreign aid. But the absence of a highly qualified civil service placed limits upon the extent and efficacy of state action. Thus, in urban areas, privately owned businesses continued to supply most local consumer goods. In agriculture, peasant proprietorship or large private estates—particularly for export products—remained the general rule.

Economic Planning In Communist Countries

Planning in the early USSR

The kind of economic planning that was practiced in the Soviet Union and in most other communist countries until the 1990s had developed during the 1920s and '30s in the struggle to industrialise the USSR. The Bolsheviks had seized power in 1917 without any clear notion as to how an economy should be run. No guidance was to be found in the writings of Karl Marx other than the assertion that a socialist society would operate the economy for the common good, which suggested that it would create organs of economic administration to replace the market system of capitalism. In the future communist society there would be no money, no profit motive. No wages would be necessary to stimulate effort. It would be "from each according to his ability, to each according to his needs." Economics, a science of exchange relationships or value, would wither away or be replaced by a kind of higher management. The Bolshevik leader N.I. Bukharin wrote in 1920:

The leader of the Bolsheviks, Vladimir Lenin, shared these somewhat utopian expectations. It is not clear from his pre-1917 writings just what kind of economic organisation he had in mind for Russia should achieve power. As it turned out, the Russian Revolution of October 1917 was accompanied by economic breakdown, a refusal of cooperation from officials and managers, civil war, and uncontrollable inflation. Partly under the stress of these circumstances, partly from ideology, the Bolsheviks moved to establish thoroughgoing state control over industry and trade, nationalised all economic property including land, declared all private enterprise illegal, and demanded that the peasants deliver all farm surpluses to state procurement organs. Money lost all value.

On paper, this period of War Communism, as it is now called, was one of centralised planning. All economic units, except the peasant producers, were subjected to orders from the government's Supreme Council of National Economy (V.S.N.Kh.). But this initial essay in planning was a failure—except insofar as it facilitated the concentration of the few available resources for the civil war fronts. Rationing functioned spasmodically, there was famine, and output fell drastically.

The controversies of the 1920s

In 1921, Lenin introduced the New Economic Policy (NEP). Small-scale private manufacturing, private trade, and free sale of peasant surpluses became legal once again, while the state retained the "commanding heights" (e.g., large-scale industry, foreign trade, banking, transport). The state sector continued to be operated under the aegis of V.S.N.Kh. by trusts and enterprises with state-appointed managers. In 1921, the State Planning Committee (Gosplan) came into existence to advise the government and its economic alter ego, the Council of Labour and Defence, but planning was still a shadowy process. Trusts and enterprises had considerable autonomy and were free to make agreements and grant credits to one another. The planners made forecasts, and government policy decisions influenced the level and direction of state investments; but there was no integrated system of production and allocation planning, even in the state sector, while the private sector was not directly planned at all. In 1924, only 35 percent of the national income, 1.5 percent of agricultural production, less than half of all retail trade, and three-quarters of industrial output were "socialised"; the rest was private.

In 1926–28, a vigorous discussion raged about the future basis of planning. Two schools of thought developed, one advocating "genetic" and the other "teleological" planning. The former, composed of the more moderate and cautious planners, believed that plans should be based on existing trends in the economy and reasonable projections thereof. The latter considered that drastic measures were necessary to speed up the industrialisation of the country, and this "teleological" school produced extremely ambitious drafts of the First Five-Year Plan. The radicals conceived the plan as taking precedence over all previous economic decisions so as to enable a sharp break with the past. With the support of the Soviet leader Joseph Stalin, it was their view that won.

The First Five-Year Plan

The First Five-Year Plan (1928–1932), which was later said to have been carried out in four years, called for immense investments in heavy industry; for example, steel output was to be more than doubled by 1932. Amid great confusion, the planning mechanism was overhauled, and gradually a "command economy" was established. In this system, subordinate units of the economy (e.g., industrial enterprises) operated in accordance with administrative instructions, and they did not decide their inputs or outputs by negotiation with other enterprises, these being determined by the planners. The sole effective criterion of management decision became conformity to plan—i.e., to the instructions issued by the central administrative planning organs. In this way, the political authorities achieved a high degree of control over resource allocation and were able to enforce their priorities. Consequently, when the First Five-Year Plan ran into trouble, the government was able to insist on the fulfillment of most of the plans for key sectors of heavy industry, at the cost of a drastic fall in availability of consumers' goods.

The structure of the Soviet planning system

A rearrangement of the planning system was the necessary consequence of the new tasks it was called upon to perform. In 1932, three People's Commissariats (for heavy, light, and timber industries) replaced the V.S.N.Kh.; these were further split, and by 1939 the industries of the USSR were run by 21 People's Commissariats (the numbers varied in subsequent years). Each commissariat (renamed ministry in 1946) controlled a branch of industry, either directly or through a ministry in one of the union republics. The ministries issued instructions to "their" enterprises, organised the supply of materials and components, and also disposed of the output.

At the apex of the system stood the leaders of the Communist Party, who decided the policy objectives in economic as in other matters and who made choices as to the means of achieving those objectives. All key appointments in the economic hierarchy were made or confirmed by appropriate party committees.

The work of Gosplan

It was Gosplan's task to "translate" the politically determined objectives into a consistent set of plan targets. There had to be coherence between production and supply at all times, as well as between investment plans and the current production of capital goods. Foreign trade also had to be taken into account, as a drain on available resources (exports) and as a source of needed goods (imports). The planners proceeded by drawing up a series of material balances, which expressed anticipated supply of, and demand for, all key commodities. The successive versions of the plan were revised until a general balance was attained, since it was no use planning an increase in production of any item if the necessary additional machinery, raw material, and fuel could not be made available. The task was of special complexity in the short term (i.e., within a period of a year), since the plan had to take the form of millions of consistent instructions to thousands of enterprises to produce, deliver, transport, and process millions of commodities of a great many shapes, sizes, and types.

Needless to say, all these decisions must be made somewhere in all economic systems. The Soviet type of "command economy" developed under Stalin, however, provided no criterion for decentralised decision making such as is provided, however imperfectly, by the market mechanism in Western capitalist countries. Consequently, the coordination of all these decisions had to be consciously achieved by the planners. In practice much depended on proposals from below, since the planners suffered from information overload. The actual plans were necessarily aggregated (e.g., tons of metal, millions of square metres of cloth, millions of rubles' worth of construction or of furniture), so that decisions on the product mix were necessarily decentralised. The resultant malfunctioning came to be much criticized in the Soviet press. Quality was often sacrificed in order to fulfill the plan in quantitative terms; planned targets expressed in tons, for example, encouraged excessive weight in the product concerned, while targets expressed in rubles discouraged economy and rewarded the use of expensive materials. Plan-fulfillment as a dominant criterion of success stimulated management to conceal their productive potential so as to get an "easy" plan, while fears of supply shortages encouraged hoarding. Soviet critics increasingly pointed to the rigidity of prices, which did not reflect supply–demand conditions. The planners claimed that it was their task not that of the price mechanism, to ensure balance between supply and demand, but the enormous complexity of their task made it impossible for them to do so.

The Gorbachev reform agenda

Low growth rates in the late 1970s and early '80s, on top of continued shortages and corruption, alarmed the Soviet leadership. Many proposals were aired as to how the system might be changed. A series of reforms were in fact promulgated (notably in 1965 and 1974), but these were soon criticized as having been inconsistent and halfhearted.

The programme of reform proposed and undertaken in the period 1987–90 under the leadership of Mikhail Gorbachev represented a truly radical change in the nature of the Soviet system, the first since the early 1930s. In this programme it was intended that the bulk of the product mix would be decided not by the planners but by management, in negotiation with their customers or with the wholesale-trade organs. The need for competition was explicitly recognised, both between state enterprises seeking customers and between them and newly legalised cooperatives (more or less free enterprises). Enterprises were to be protected by law against arbitrary exactions by their superiors. An end was decreed to "soft" credits and subsidies, leaving open the real possibility of bankruptcy. Large enterprises were to be allowed direct access to foreign markets.

Reforms along these lines were gradually introduced, but some formidable obstacles proved impossible to surmount. One was chronic shortage, which continued to stimulate hoarding and compelled the continuation of material allocation. Prices were only slowly and with difficulty reformed. The declared aim of speeding up growth led to the survival of growth targets, in the familiar units of rubles, tons, and square metres, although the reformers aimed to abolish such targets. The priority of centrally determined objectives was assured by the system of so-called gos-zakazy (state orders), and these could cover the major part of the output of many enterprises. There were, moreover, serious problems of ideology (the enhanced role of the market came into conflict with traditional Marxist views) and bureaucratic resistance. Deeper reforms that were proposed threatened the fundamental powers of the Communist Party and its officials. In the meantime, the central government watched its authority over economic decision making steadily erode at the republic and regional levels, largely owing to Gorbachev's more liberal policies. Central economic planning ceased to have any meaning as many enterprises, effectively freed from government oversight, tried to cope in an economy that as yet lacked the free play of market mechanisms. With the collapse of the Soviet central government in late 1991, economic policy-making devolved upon Russia and the other newly independent republics of the former union, most of whom appeared committed to a diversified economic structure in which central planning would play a much-reduced role.

Soviet agricultural planning

Agricultural planning in the Soviet Union had a peculiarly difficult history. With priority given to industrialisation, agriculture during the regime of Stalin was essentially treated as a source of cheap food and materials for the cities. The peasants were, in fact, expropriated by force in the period 1930–35, and the bulk of them were compelled to join collective farms (kolkhozy). While in Soviet ideology state farms, operated like factories with wage labour, were preferred to collective farms, they remained of relatively minor importance until after 1954. Mechanisation was for many years confined to a very few crops and especially to grain growing. The entire system was primarily designed to ensure deliveries of produce at low prices, and the planners and administrators concentrated on procurements, while production plans were seldom, if ever, fulfilled. Under Nikita Khrushchev in the late 1950s and early 1960s there was a substantial change of policy, with greatly improved prices and a major investment programme designed to restore agriculture to health.

This policy was continued under Leonid Brezhnev in the 1960s and '70s. Despite very large investments and higher farm prices, however, output rose slowly and costs rose quickly, necessitating very large subsidies. Peasant incomes rose, but incentives to work on the large state and collective farms were ineffective, and millions of townspeople had to be mobilised annually to help with the harvest. An important reform was the spread within state and collective farms of the use of autonomous work groups that were paid according to results. In 1987, proposals were adopted that would allow the leasing of land to families over and above the small plots and privately owned livestock that most rural residents had and that even as late as 1986 were producing 25 percent of the Soviet Union's entire agricultural output.

As the authority of the central government crumbled in 1990–91, many state and collective farms gained de facto control over their own affairs, though few used this to any distinct advantage. More profound changes seemed likely as a result of the breakup of the Soviet Union in 1991 and would probably involve the reversion of farmlands to private ownership in some republics.

Planning in other communist countries

In other communist-ruled countries the Soviet system was extensively copied, even in minor details, until 1956. After that date much depended on choices made by the party leadership of each country. Both Yugoslavia (in the 1960s) and China (in the 1980s) decentralised control over major sectors of their economies and introduced individual incentives on a significant scale. The Soviet Union's satellites in Eastern Europe, by contrast, maintained fairly rigid centralised controls until 1989–90. At that time, the Soviets abandoned their political-military control over the region, and most eastern European countries used the opportunity to begin moving toward a free-market economic system, however haltingly and even painfully.

Poland

Poland's unsound economic policies in the 1970s led to serious domestic imbalances and a growing foreign debt and contributed to the political-economic crisis of 1980–81. Martial law, imposed in 1981, made possible the imposition of a very sharp rise in consumer prices, and the regime then adopted a radical reform designed to greatly strengthen the market mechanism. Its implementation, however, was delayed by the chronic shortages and imbalances inherited from the previous period. It is noteworthy that the bulk of agriculture in Poland remained dominated by private peasant smallholders, who were free to sell what and when they wished. Beginning in 1990, the new post-communist government of Poland abandoned price controls and subsidies and undertook a major currency reform in a drastic programme to convert the Polish economy to a free-market basis. The privatisation of the larger state-owned enterprises proceeded relatively slowly, however, as in other eastern European countries.

Czechoslovakia

Czechoslovakia's centralised economic system was in the process of being reformed in 1968, when fears of more fundamental political change brought about Soviet military intervention, which had the side effect of halting the economic reform process. Following the events of 1989–90, Czechoslovakia moved in the same general direction as Poland. State subsidies on many items were reduced, prices were decontrolled, and the private ownership of industrial and commercial enterprises and of farmland was legalised and even encouraged. Larger industrial enterprises were converted to joint-stock companies, and their shares were sold to the public.

East Germany

East Germany's industrial planning was based upon a set of monopolistic cartels (Kombinate), which had considerable autonomy in carrying out the tasks of satisfying the needs of domestic customers and of export markets. Perhaps because of traditional German organisational skills and work ethic, the system was more efficient in operation than those of most other countries in the Soviet bloc. It remained woefully inefficient by the standards of the free-market economies of Western Europe, however, as became clear following West Germany's historic unification with East Germany in 1990. When deprived of their state subsidies, most eastern German industries proved unable to survive in free competition with those of western Germany or with other European Community countries. As a result, eastern Germany's rapidly shrinking industrial sector quickly came to depend on subsidies from the German government and on massive new plant investment by corporations based in western Germany.

Romania

Of all the Soviet-bloc nations, it was Romania that most fully retained Stalinist methods, both in the economy and in politics, into the 1970s and '80s. Unsound economic policies led to a long-lived situation of crisis and acute shortages, especially of energy and even of food. The resulting widespread deprivation sparked a popular uprising in 1989 that overthrew Romania's longtime leader, Nicolae Ceausescu. But, as in some other eastern European nations, the end of communist rule in Romania was followed by a sharp economic decline: the closing of unprofitable state-supported industries resulted in falling production and rising unemployment, while shortages of food and other consumer goods continued and even worsened.

Hungary

In 1968, Hungary adopted a system of market socialism that left each enterprise management very largely free to determine its own production programme. The central planners were no longer to set obligatory production targets. While some prices remained controlled, others were set free. Enterprises were also given some freedom to buy and sell abroad, and efforts were made to link Hungarian prices with those on world markets. Profits became the principal measure of managerial success, and bonuses based on profits had an appreciable effect on managers' and workers' incomes. Large-scale investments were still controlled by the central planners, but the enterprises were required to finance roughly 40 percent of all investments out of their own resources.

Balance of payments difficulties and internal pressures (e.g., for subsidies to unsuccessful enterprises), however, led to severe strains, and output and living standards stagnated after 1978. Agriculture, however, dominated by genuinely autonomous cooperatives and a flourishing private sector, continued to do well. Hungary also had a sizable "second economy," with a variety of legal small-scale private enterprises.

Yugoslavia

The Yugoslav communists developed their own conception of socialist planning after their break with Moscow in 1948. The collectivisation of agriculture was abandoned in the early 1950s. The control of the state-owned enterprises was given to workers' councils that would decide their own production programmes according to profitability, with prices subject to negotiation. Investments were partly controlled by the enterprises themselves out of profits or by the central planners, partly financed from bank credits. But lack of effective central control, and rivalries between national republics, gave rise in the 1980s to a serious economic crisis led by a rapidly rising rate of inflation. These economic difficulties foreshadowed Yugoslavia's breakup in the early 1990s.

China

Chinese communist planning at first followed the Soviet pattern. In 1958, however, came the Great Leap Forward, an effort to speed up progress by shifting rural manpower into manufacturing. This failed disastrously, and the Chinese communist leadership had to devise its own planning methods, adapted to a vast country with poor communications and a low stage of economic development. After the social-political cataclysm known as the Cultural Revolution and the death of Mao Zedong, reformers led by Deng Xiaoping came to power in the late 1970s and launched a major shake-up of the system. Agriculture was decollectivised, small-scale private trade and workshops were legalised, and the role of market forces was substantially increased. Larger-scale industry remained subject to central planning controls, though there too market-type reforms were experimented with. While there were successes, balance of payments problems and inflationary pressures continued to cause some anxiety. Agricultural output rose sharply at first, but concern over shortfalls in cereals production continued. In China too the search went on for the elusive optimal balance between plan and market.

Assessment of Soviet-type planning

The Soviet type of planning grew up under the special conditions prevailing in the USSR and was adapted to the task of speedy industrialisation of a poor country, with strong emphasis on heavy industry, explicable partly by the logic of industrialisation (steel and machinery are more conducive to industrial growth than textiles and jam), partly by concern for military potential. The system made it easy for the authorities to attain a high rate of forced saving and investment and a rapid buildup of basic industries, though at the cost of neglecting for many years the elementary needs of the citizens. Insofar as the investment plans of most basic industries depended in the last resort on a quantitative estimate of future demand, the Soviet system was reasonably well adapted to making such estimates, since so much of the additional demand was a consequence of the planners' own decisions.

In practice, of course, Soviet-type planning was not always able to realise these potential advantages. There were repeated instances of overinvestment, followed by the abandonment or freezing of partly finished projects. Experience also showed that the separate administrative units into which a nationalised economy must be divided can take as narrow and short-term a view as any capitalist entrepreneur. Thus, the most easily accessible forests were cut, the richest sources of iron ore exhausted, and fallow land put under the plow in order to fulfill current plans, with little consideration of the consequences. A centralised system of material balances is not insurance against erroneous forecasting. The material-balances approach exercised a conservative influence, perhaps because it was simplest to plan on the assumption that the various technical coefficients would remain constant. Innovation was often resisted, and the influence of user demand was weak. It must be borne in mind, of course, that Western economies also have many imperfections. A theoretical model of centralised planning works as smoothly and as efficiently as a theoretical model of a perfectly competitive market, but neither exists in the real world.

Following the death of Stalin in 1953, the Soviet economic system was presented with new problems. It showed itself unable to cope effectively with the finer adjustments required in a sophisticated industrial economy. In particular, the system was not able to stimulate the adoption of new technology despite heavy expenditure on research. It dealt very clumsily with the satisfaction of consumer demand, though this became more important in the changed political conditions, not only in the Soviet Union but also in most of its European allies. The unsuitability of the traditional Soviet planning model in a modern, highly technological, and intensely competitive world economy became painfully clear to the generation of Soviet leaders who came to power in the mid-1980s. But their efforts to incorporate with socialist planning the flexibility and grass-roots enterprise that come with market mechanisms also failed, largely because central planning had become indissolubly tied to the totalitarian structure of state power in the Soviet Union.

Economic Planning in Noncommunist Countries

Planning in developed countries: origins and objectives

Since the end of World War II in 1945, most noncommunist developed countries have practiced some explicit form of economic plan. Such countries include Belgium, Canada, Finland, France, Germany, Ireland, Italy, Japan, the Netherlands, New Zealand, Norway, Portugal, Spain, Sweden, and the United Kingdom. Planning as a focus for economic policy-making in these countries had its heyday in the 1960s and '70s.

After that time, although the formal mechanisms for working up the national economic plan remained in existence, their impact upon national economic policy-making was much diminished. Governments harboured narrower ambitions, and public opinion came to expect less from government action.

Origins of planning

Until World War II there was no serious attempt at economic planning outside the Soviet Union. During the Great Depression of the 1930s, many governments were forced to intervene vigorously in economic affairs, but in a manner that amounted to economic warfare; this intervention took the form of giving increased protection to domestic producers against competition from abroad; of acquiescing in the formation of cartels and other arrangements among producers to raise prices and reduce competition; and of higher levels of government spending, some of it for relief and some of it for armaments.

At the end of the war there was a shift to the left in the politics of some of the countries, and with it a turn to more positive forms of government intervention. In Great Britain the Labour Party secured a large majority in Parliament in 1945, and with it a mandate for policies aiming at more social equality. In Scandinavia, particularly in Sweden, moderate left-wing traditions in government made a transition to planning politically acceptable. In France, left-wing groups, including the Communist Party, emerged as the dominant political force after 1945 with programmes of far-reaching social reform. More important, a group of eminent public servants, engineers, and business leaders—continuing a tradition of French 19th-century capitalism known as Saint-Simonianism—were in favour of the state taking a leading role in economic affairs.

While the initial impulse to planning came from the political left, actual decisions by governments to plan were based on practical considerations rather than on political doctrine. The decision to plan most often followed a crisis in a country's economic affairs, as was the case in France after World War II, when there was an urgent need to reconstruct and modernise the economy. In the United Kingdom the setting up of a medium-term plan accompanied the emergency measures taken to deal with a balance of payments crisis in July 1961; and the Labour government's National Plan of September 1965 was formulated in similar circumstances. In Belgium and Ireland, dissatisfaction with the past performance of the economy was a major reason for planning. Belgium had not shared in the European prosperity of the 1950s, and accordingly, in 1959, the government adopted a plan aimed at an increase of 4 percent a year in the GNP, practically double the rate achieved from 1955 to 1960. Its planning methods were modeled on those of France.

The French example also influenced planning in other European countries. In Great Britain a Conservative government undertook, during a balance of payments crisis in July 1961, to set up a National Economic Development Council to draft a five-year economic plan that would emphasise much more rapid economic growth. The Netherlands, which had been very successful since the war in achieving balanced economic growth, initiated five-year plans in 1963 through the medium of the Central Planning Bureau, which had for some years been advising on national budgetary policies. Italy had first turned to planning in the 1950s, when a plan for the development of southern Italy was launched; later, attempts were made to extend this example of regional economic planning into a plan for the national economy. Even in West Germany, where the Christian Democratic governments had emphasised a policy of strengthening the free market, a need for some central management of the economy was increasingly recognised.

Economic planning in the developed countries has always been pragmatic rather than inspired by an attempt to apply preconceived ideological doctrines. In the 1980s, governments in most of these countries swung to the right of the political pendulum and were therefore less sympathetic to the idea of economic planning, which therefore took a back seat in national economic policy-making. The problems that the developed countries faced (chiefly slow growth and high unemployment) were thought not to be amenable to more state action. Indeed, the cost of financing government was thought in influential circles to be stifling private initiative. In the same way, many enterprises under public ownership were "privatised" (that is, returned to private ownership), and the scope of government regulation of the economy was notably reduced. In the view of a new generation of policymakers, the major role of government in promoting economic growth was, first, to provide a stable, noninflationary framework for enterprises to make their decisions and, second, to support the emergence of the new "information society" through improved education and technical training and research and development programmes.

Objectives of planning

The plans drafted in the developed countries postulate target rates of growth and some indication of the choices to be made in allocating rates of increase to the various kinds of expenditures on available goods and services (private and public consumption, social investment, directly productive investment, stocks, and exports). Further, as the plan has to be balanced, the total of these components of overall demand must fall within the probable total available supply of goods and services, after allowing for the desired level of the current balance of payments surplus. The rates of increase of some types of demand—directly productive investment and stocks in particular—are fixed within fairly narrow limits by technological considerations once the overall rate of growth of output has been chosen. But an important area of choice concerns the respective rates of growth of private consumption by individuals and what has come to be called collective consumption—e.g., education, health, urban facilities, provision for culture.

Another planning objective that has become very prominent (and that figures in the plans of Great Britain, the Netherlands, France, and Italy, to mention only a few) is the correction of imbalances in regional development.

One of the most important functions of economic planning is to achieve consistency among different economic objectives. Some desirable goals are likely to conflict with others. While it may be possible, for example, to stimulate the economy so as to obtain sharply higher levels of output and employment, the measures required to do this may also produce rapidly rising prices, which in turn will lead to rising imports and falling exports; the result may be a balance of payments crisis.

Chapter - 2

Five-Year Plans of India

From 1947 to 2017, the Indian economy was premised on the concept of planning. This was carried through the Five-Year Plans, developed, executed, and monitored by the Planning Commission (1951-2014) and the NITI Aayog (2015-2017). With the prime minister as the ex-officio chairman, the commission has a nominated deputy chairman, who holds the rank of a cabinet minister. Montek Singh Ahluwalia is the last deputy chairman of the commission (resigned on 26 May 2014). The Twelfth Plan completed its term in March 2017. Prior to the Fourth Plan, the allocation of state resources was based on schematic patterns rather than a transparent and objective mechanism, which led to the adoption of the Gadgil formula in 1969. Revised versions of the formula have been used since then to determine the allocation of central assistance for state plans. The new government led by Narendra Modi, elected in 2014, has announced the dissolution of the Planning Commission, and its replacement by a think tank called the NITI Aayog (an acronym for National Institution for Transforming India).

History

Programs

Joseph Stalin implemented the First Five-Year Plan in the Soviet Union in 1928. Most communist states and several capitalist countries subsequently have adopted them. China continues to use FYPs, although China renamed its Eleventh FYP, from 2006 to 2010, a guideline (geisha), rather than a plan (jihua), to signify the central government's more hands-off approach to development. India launched its First FYP in 1951, immediately after independence, under the socialist influence of India's first prime minister, Jawaharlal Nehru.

The First Five-Year Plan was one of the most important, because it had a great role in the launching of Indian development after Independence. Thus, it strongly supported agriculture production and also launched the industrialisation of the country (but less than the Second Plan, which focused on heavy industries). It built a particular system of mixed economy, with a great role for the public sector (with an emerging welfare state), as well as a growing private sector (represented by some personalities as those who published the Bombay Plan).

First Plan (1951–1956)

The first Indian Prime Minister, Jawaharlal Nehru, presented the First Five-Year Plan to the Parliament of India and needed urgent attention. The First Five-year Plan was launched in 1951 which mainly focused in development of the primary sector. The First Five-Year Plan was based on the Harrod–Domar model with few modifications.

The total planned budget of Rs, 2069 crore (2378 crore later) was allocated to seven broad areas: irrigation and energy (27.2%), agriculture and community development(17.4%), transport and communications (24%), industry (8.4%), social services (16.6%), rehabilitation of landless farmers (4.1%), and for other sectors and services (2.5%). The most important feature of this phase was active role of state in all economic sectors. Such a role was justified at that time because immediately after independence, India was facing basic problems—deficiency of capital and low capacity to save.

The target growth rate was 2.1% annual gross domestic product (GDP) growth; the achieved growth rate was 3.6% the net domestic product went up by 15%. The monsoon was good and there were relatively high crop yields, boosting exchange reserves and the per capita income, which increased by 8%. National income increased more than the per capita income due to rapid population growth. Many irrigation projects were initiated during this period, including the Bhakra, Hirakud, Mettur Dam and Damodar Valley dams. The World Health Organisation (WHO), with the Indian government, addressed children's health and reduced infant mortality, indirectly contributing to population growth.

At the end of the plan period in 1956, five Indian Institutes of Technology (IITs) were started as major technical institutions.

The University Grants Commission (UGC) was set up to take care of funding and take measures to strengthen the higher education in the country. Contracts were signed to start five steel plants, which came into existence in the middle of the Second Five-Year Plan. The plan was quasi-successful for the government.

Second Plan (1956–1961)

The Second Plan focused on the development of the public sector and rapid Industrialization. The plan followed the Mahalanobis model, an economic development model developed by the Indian statistician Prasanta Chandra Mahalanobis in 1953. The plan attempted to determine the optimal allocation of investment between productive sectors in order to maximise long-run economic growth. It used the prevalent state-of-the-art techniques of operations research and optimisation as well as the novel applications of statistical models developed at the Indian Statistical Institute. The plan assumed a closed economy in which the main trading activity would be centre on importing capital goods.

Hydroelectric power projects and five steel plants at Bhilai, Durgapur, and Rourkela were established with the help of Russia, Britain (the UK) and West Germany respectively. Coal production was increased. More railway lines were added in the north-east.

The Tata Institute of Fundamental Research and Atomic Energy Commission of India were established as research institutes. In 1957, a talent search and scholarship programme was begun to find talented young students to train for work in nuclear power.

The total amount allocated under the Second Five-Year Plan in India was ₹ 48 billion. This amount was allocated among various sectors: power and irrigation, social services, communications and transport, and miscellaneous. The second plan was a period of rising prices. The country also faced foreign exchange crisis. The rapid growth in population slowed down the growth in the per capita income.

The target growth rate was 4.5% and the actual growth rate was 4.27%.

The plan was criticised by classical liberal economist B.R. Shenoy who noted that the plan's . Shenoy argued that state control of the economy would undermine a young democracy. India faced an external payments crisis in 1957, which is viewed as confirmation of Shenoy's argument.

Third Plan (1961–1966)

The Third Five-Year Plan stressed agriculture and improvement in the production of wheat, but the brief Sino-Indian War of 1962 exposed weaknesses in the economy and shifted the focus towards the defence industry and the Indian Army. In 1965–1966, India fought a War with Pakistan. There was also a severe drought in 1965. The war led to inflation and the priority was shifted to price stabilisation. The construction of dams continued. Many cement and fertiliser plants were also built. Punjab began producing an abundance of wheat.

Many primary schools were started in rural areas. In an effort to bring democracy to the grass-root level, Panchayat elections were started and the states were given more development responsibilities.

State electricity boards and state secondary education boards were formed. States were made responsible for secondary and higher education. State road transportation corporations were formed and local road building became a state responsibility.

The target growth rate was 5.6%, but the actual growth rate was 2.4%.

Plan Holidays (1966–1969)

Due to miserable failure of the Third Plan the government was forced to declare "plan holidays" (from 1966–67, 1967–68, and 1968–69). Three annual plans were drawn during this intervening period. During 1966–67 there was again the problem of drought. Equal priority was given to agriculture, its allied activities, and industrial sector. The government of India declared "Devaluation of Rupee" to increase the exports of the country. The main reasons for plan holidays were the war, lack of resources and increase in inflation.

Fourth Plan (1969–1974)

At this time Indira Gandhi was the prime minister. The Indira Gandhi government nationalised 14 major Indian banks and the Green Revolution in India advanced agriculture. In addition, the situation in

East Pakistan (now Bangladesh) was becoming dire as the Indo-Pakistan War of 1971 and Bangladesh Liberation War took funds earmarked for industrial development. India also performed the Smiling Buddha underground nuclear test (Pokhran-1) in Rajasthan on May 18, 1974, partially in response to the United States deployment of the Seventh Fleet in the Bay of Bengal. The fleet had been deployed to warn India against attacking West Pakistan and extending the war.

The target growth rate was 5.6%, but the actual growth rate was 3.3%.

Fifth Plan (1974–1978)

The Fifth Five-Year Plan laid stress on employment, poverty alleviation (Garibi Hatao), and justice. The plan also focused on self-reliance in agricultural production and defence. In 1978, the newly elected Morarji Desai government rejected the plan. The Electricity Supply Act was amended in 1975, which enabled the central government to enter into power generation and transmission.

The Indian national highway system was introduced and many roads were widened to accommodate the increasing traffic. Tourism also expanded. The twenty-point programme was launched in 1975. It was followed from 1974 to 1979.

The Minimum Needs Programme (MNP) was introduced in the first year of the Fifth Five-Year Plan (1974–78). The objective of the programme is to provide certain basic minimum needs and thereby improve the living standards of the people. It is prepared and launched by D.P. Dhar.

The target growth rate was 4.4% and the actual growth rate was 4.8%.

Rolling Plan (1978–1980)

The Janata Party government rejected the Fifth Five-Year Plan and introduced a new Sixth Five-Year Plan (1978–1980). This plan was again rejected by the Indian National Congress government in 1980 and a new Sixth Plan was made. The Rolling Plan consisted of three kinds of plans that were proposed. The First Plan was for the present year which comprised the annual budget and the Second was a plan for a fixed number of years, which may be 3, 4 or 5 years. The Second Plan kept changing as per the requirements of the Indian economy. The Third Plan was a perspective plan for long terms i.e. for 10, 15 or 20 years. Hence there was no fixation of dates for the commencement and termination of the plan in the rolling plans. The main advantage of the rolling plans was that they were flexible and were able to overcome the rigidity of fixed Five-Year Plans by mending targets, the object of the exercise, projections and allocations as per the changing conditions in the country's economy. The main disadvantage of this plan was that if the targets were revised each year, it became difficult to achieve the targets laid down in the five-year period and it turned out to be a complex plan. Also, the frequent revisions resulted in the lack of stability in the economy.

Sixth Plan (1980–1985)

The Sixth Five-Year Plan marked the beginning of economic liberalisation. Price controls were eliminated and ration shops were closed. This led to an increase in food prices and an increase in the cost of living. This was the end of Nehruvian socialism. The National Bank for Agriculture and Rural Development was established for development of rural areas on 12 July 1982 by recommendation of the Shivaraman Committee. Family planning was also expanded in order to prevent overpopulation. In contrast to China's strict and binding one-child policy, Indian policy did not rely on the threat of force. More prosperous areas of India adopted family planning more rapidly than less prosperous areas, which continued to have a high birth rate. Military Five-Year Plans became coterminous with Planning Commission's plans from this plan onwards.

The Sixth Five-Year Plan was a great success to the Indian economy. The target growth rate was 5.2% and the actual growth rate was 5.7%.

Seventh Plan (1985–1990)

The Seventh Five-Year Plan was led by the Congress Party with Rajiv Gandhi as the prime minister. The plan laid stress on improving the productivity level of industries by upgrading of technology.

The main objectives of the Seventh Five-Year Plan were to establish growth in areas of increasing economic productivity, production of food grains, and generating employment through "Social Justice".

As an outcome of the Sixth Five-Year Plan, there had been steady growth in agriculture, controls on the rate of inflation, and favourable balance of payments which had provided a strong base for the Seventh Five-Year Plan to build on the need for further economic growth. The Seventh Plan had strived towards socialism and energy production at large. The thrust areas of the Seventh Five-Year Plan were: social justice, removal of oppression of the weak, using modern technology, agricultural development, anti-poverty programmes, full supply of food, clothing, and shelter, increasing productivity of small- and large-scale farmers, and making India an independent economy.

Based on a 15-year period of striving towards steady growth, the Seventh Plan was focused on achieving the prerequisites of self-sustaining growth by the year 2000. The plan expected the labour force to grow by 39 million people and employment was expected to grow at the rate of 4% per year.

Some of the expected outcomes of the Seventh Five-Year Plan India are given below:

- Balance of payments (estimates): Export – ₹ 330 billion (US$4.6 billion), Imports – (-) ₹ 540 billion (US$7.6 billion), Trade Balance – (-) ₹ 210 billion (US$2.9 billion)
- Merchandise exports (estimates): ₹ 606.53 billion (US$8.5 billion).
- Merchandise imports (estimates): ₹ 954.37 billion (US$13.4 billion).
- Projections for balance of payments: Export – ₹ 607 billion (US$8.5 billion), Imports – (-) ₹ 954 billion (US$13.4 billion), Trade Balance- (-) ₹ 347 billion (US$4.9 billion)

Under the Seventh Five-Year Plan, India strove to bring about a self-sustained economy in the country with valuable contributions from voluntary agencies and the general populace.

The target growth rate was 5.0% and the actual growth rate was 6.01% and the growth rate of per capita income was 3.7%.

Annual Plans (1990–1992)

The Eighth Plan could not take off in 1990 due to the fast changing economic situation at the centre and the years 1990–91 and

1991–92 were treated as Annual Plans. The Eighth Plan was finally formulated for the period 1992–1997.

Eighth Plan (1992–1997)

1989–91 was a period of economic instability in India and hence no Five-Year Plan was implemented. Between 1990 and 1992, there were only Annual Plans. In 1991, India faced a crisis in foreign exchange (forex) reserves, left with reserves of only about US$.1.8 billion. Thus, under pressure, the country took the risk of reforming the socialist economy. P.V. Narasimha Rao was the ninth prime minister of the Republic of India and head of Congress Party, and led one of the most important administrations in India's modern history, overseeing a major economic transformation and several incidents affecting national security. At that time Dr. Manmohan Singh (later prime minister of India) launched India's free market reforms that brought the nearly bankrupt nation back from the edge. It was the beginning of liberalisation, privatisation and globalisation (LPG) in India.

Modernisation of industries was a major highlight of the Eighth Plan. Under this plan, the gradual opening of the Indian economy was undertaken to correct the burgeoning deficit and foreign debt. Meanwhile, India became a member of the World Trade Organisation on 1 January 1995. The major objectives included, controlling population growth, poverty reduction, employment generation, strengthening the infrastructure, institutional building, tourism management, human resource development, involvement of Panchayat raj, Nagar Palikas, NGOs, decentralisation and people's participation.

Energy was given priority with 26.6% of the outlay.

The target growth rate was 5.6% and the actual growth rate was 6.8%.

To achieve the target of an average of 5.6% per annum, investment of 23.2% of the gross domestic product was required. The incremental capital ratio is 4.1. The saving for investment was to come from domestic sources and foreign sources, with the rate of domestic saving at 21.6% of gross domestic production and of foreign saving at 1.6% of gross domestic production.

Ninth Plan (1997–2002)

The Ninth Five-Year Plan came after 50 years of Indian Independence. Atal Bihari Vajpayee was the prime minister of India during the Ninth Plan. The Ninth Plan tried primarily to use the latent and unexplored economic potential of the country to promote economic and social growth. It offered strong support to the social spheres of the country in an effort to achieve the complete elimination of poverty. The satisfactory implementation of the Eighth Five-Year Plan also ensured the states' ability to proceed on the path of faster development. The Ninth Five-Year Plan also saw joint efforts from the public and the private sectors in ensuring economic development of the country. In addition, the Ninth Five-Year Plan saw contributions towards development from the general public as well as governmental agencies in both the rural and urban areas of the country. New implementation measures in the form of Special Action Plans (SAPs) were evolved during the Ninth Plan to fulfill targets within the stipulated time with adequate resources. The SAPs covered the areas of social infrastructure, agriculture, information technology and Water policy.

Budget

The Ninth Five-Year Plan had a total public sector plan outlay of Rs 859,200 crore (US$120 billion). The Ninth Five-Year Plan also saw a hike of 48% in terms of plan expenditure and 33% in terms of the plan outlay in comparison to that of the Eighth Five-Year Plan. In the total outlay, the share of the center was approximately 57% while it was 43% for the states and the union territories.

The Ninth Five-Year Plan focused on the relationship between the rapid economic growth and the quality of life for the people of the country. The prime focus of this plan was to increase growth in the country with an emphasis on social justice and equity. The Ninth Five-Year Plan placed considerable importance on combining growth oriented policies with the mission of achieving the desired objective of improving policies which would work towards the improvement of the poor in the country. The Ninth Plan also aimed at correcting the historical inequalities which were still prevalent in the society.

Objectives

The main objective of the Ninth Five-Year Plan was to correct historical inequalities and increase the economic growth in the country. Other aspects which constituted the Ninth Five-Year Plan were:

- Population control.
- Generating employment by giving priority to agriculture and rural development.
- Reduction of poverty.
- Ensuring proper availability of food and water for the poor.
- Availability of primary health-care facilities and other basic necessities.
- Primary education to all children in the country.
- Empowering the socially disadvantaged classes like Scheduled Castes, Scheduled Tribes and other backward classes.
- Developing self-reliance in terms of agriculture.
- Acceleration in the growth rate of the economy with the help of stable prices.

Strategies

- Structural transformations and developments in the Indian economy.
- New initiatives and initiation of corrective steps to meet the challenges in the economy of the country.
- Efficient use of scarce resources to ensure rapid growth.
- Combination of public and private support to increase employment.
- Enhancing high rates of export to achieve self-reliance.
- Providing services like electricity, telecommunication, railways etc.
- Special plans to empower the socially disadvantaged classes of the country.
- Involvement and participation of Panchayati Raj institutions/ bodies and Nagar Palikas in the development process.

Performance

- The Ninth Five-Year Plan achieved a GDP growth rate of 5.4% against a target of 6.5%

- The agriculture industry grew at a rate of 2.1% against the target of 4.2%.
- The industrial growth in the country was 4.5% which was higher than that of the target of 3%.
- The service industry had a growth rate of 7.8%.
- An average annual growth rate of 6.7% was reached.

The Ninth Five-Year Plan looks through the past weaknesses in order to frame the new measures for the overall socio-economic development of the country. However, for a well-planned economy of any country, there should be a combined participation of the governmental agencies along with the general population of that nation. A combined effort of public, private, and all levels of government is essential for ensuring the growth of India's economy.

The target growth was 7.1% and the actual growth was 6.8%.

Tenth Plan (2002–2007)

The main objectives of the Tenth Five-Year Plan:

- Attain 8% GDP growth per year.
- Reduction of poverty rate by 5% by 2007.
- Providing gainful and high-quality employment at least to the addition to the labour force.
- Reduction in gender gaps in literacy and wage rates by at least 50% by 2007.
- 20-point programme was introduced.
- Target growth: 8.1% – growth achieved: 7.7%.
- The Tenth Plan was expected to follow a regional approach rather than sectoral approach to bring down regional inequalities.
- Expenditure of ₹ 43,825 crore (US$6.1 billion) for tenth five years.

Out of total plan outlay, ₹ 921,291 crore (US$130 billion) (57.9%) was for central government and ₹ 691,009 crore (US$97 billion) (42.1%) was for states and union territories.

Eleventh Plan (2007–2012)

- It was in the period of Manmohan Singh as the prime minister.
- It aimed to increase the enrolment in higher education of 18–23 years of age group by 2011–12.
- It focused on distant education, convergence of formal, non-formal, distant and IT education institutions.
- Rapid and inclusive growth (poverty reduction).
- Emphasis on social sector and delivery of service therein.
- Empowerment through education and skill development.
- Reduction of gender inequality.
- Environmental sustainability.
- To increase the growth rate in agriculture, industry and services to 4%, 10% and 9% respectively.
- Reduce total fertility rate to 2.1.
- Provide clean drinking water for all by 2009.
- Increase agriculture growth to 4%.

Twelfth Plan (2012–2017)

The Twelfth Five-Year Plan of the Government of India has been decided to achieve a growth rate of 8.2% but the National Development Council (NDC) on 27 December 2012 approved a growth rate of 8% for the Twelfth Plan.

With the deteriorating global situation, the Deputy Chairman of the Planning Commission Montek Singh Ahluwalia has said that achieving an average growth rate of 9 percent in the next five years is not possible. The Final growth target has been set at 8% by the endorsement of the plan at the National Development Council meeting held in New Delhi.

"It is not possible to think of an average of 9% [in the Twelfth Plan]. I think somewhere between 8 and 8.5 percent is feasible," Ahluwalia said on the sidelines of a conference of State Planning Boards and departments. The approached paper for the Twelfth Plan, approved last year, talked about an annual average growth rate of 9%.

"When I say feasible... that will require major effort. If you don't do that, there is no God given right to grow at 8 percent. I think given that the world economy deteriorated very sharply over the last year...the growth rate in the first year of the 12th Plan (2012–13) is 6.5 to 7 percent."

He also indicated that soon he should share his views with other members of the Commission to choose a final number (economic growth target) to put before the country's NDC for its approval.

The government intends to reduce poverty by 10% during the 12th Five-Year Plan. Ahluwalia said, "We aim to reduce poverty estimates by 9% annually on a sustainable basis during the Plan period". Earlier, addressing a conference of State Planning Boards and Planning departments, he said the rate of decline in poverty doubled during the Eleventh Plan. The commission had said, while using the Tendulkar poverty line, the rate of reduction in the five years between 2004–05 and 2009–10, was about 1.5% points each year, which was twice that when compared to the period between 1993–95 to 2004–05. The plan aims towards the betterment of the infrastructural projects of the nation avoiding all types of bottlenecks. The document presented by the planning commission is aimed to attract private investments of up to US$1 trillion in the infrastructural growth in the 12th five-year plan, which will also ensure a reduction in the subsidy burden of the government to 1.5 percent from 2 percent of the GDP (gross domestic product). The UID (Unique Identification Number) will act as a platform for cash transfer of the subsidies in the plan.

The objectives of the Twelfth Five-Year Plan were:

- To create 50 million new work opportunities in the non-farm sector.
- To remove gender and social gap in school enrolment.
- To enhance access to higher education.
- To reduce malnutrition among children aged 0–3 years.
- To provide electricity to all villages.
- To ensure that 50% of the rural population have accesses to proper drinking water.
- To increase green cover by 1 million hectare every year.
- To provide access to banking services to 90% of households.

Future

With the Planning Commission dissolved, no more formal plans are made for the economy, but Five-Year Defence Plans continue to be made. The latest is 2017–2022. There will be no Thirteenth Five-Year Plan.

Chapter - 3

Agriculture Sector

Agriculture is the primary production sector in India: On Independence in 1947, agriculture was in very poor condition. Per acre agriculture production was very low and the irrigation projects were not in existence. Agriculture depended entirely on the vagaries of monsoon which was volatile. Some years there were droughts and some year there were heavy rains resulting in floods and entire crop production was heavily damaged.

In order to improve agriculture production, the Central and State Governments had to spent huge amounts of financial funds. Old method of cultivation need to be abandoned and new methods were necessary to be introduced. Cultivation methods were to be improved and modern machinery such as tractors need to be introduced for cultivation.

Farmers were required to be provided with improved fertilisers and seeds and tractors for cultivation at concessional rates. Agriculture production was depended on vagaries on Monsoon and in case of failure of agriculture production, the farmers were required to get financial assistance in the form of waiver of their debts and compensate for the lack of income to be received on account of failure of crops. This was the most routine exercise and the government had to pay about 500 crores per year for this purpose in addition to the import of the foodgrains from abroad. Farmers used to commit suicides in case of failure of crops as they were completely ruined. In order to avoid this, large amount was spent for compensation. Investment in agriculture subsidies were very huge but the agriculture production increased tremendously from 80 million tons in 1965 to

277 million tons in 2019 foodgrains. Large subsidies were provided by the Government of India for agriculture.

History of **agriculture in India** dates back to Indus Valley Civilisation. India ranks second worldwide in farm outputs. As per 2018, agriculture employed more than 50% of the Indian work force and contributed 17–18% to country's GDP. According to latest report, agriculture is primary source of livelihood for 58% population in India.

In 2016, agriculture and allied sectors like animal husbandry, forestry and fisheries accounted for 15.4% of the GDP (gross domestic product) with about 31% of the workforce in 2014. India ranks first in the world with highest net cropped area followed by US and China. The economic contribution of agriculture to India's GDP is steadily declining with the country's broad-based economic growth. Still, agriculture is demographically the broadest economic sector and plays a significant role in the overall socio-economic fabric of India. India exported $38 billion worth of agricultural products in 2013, making it the seventh largest agricultural exporter worldwide and the sixth largest net exporter. Most of its agriculture exports serve developing and least developed nations. Indian agricultural/horticultural and processed foods are exported to more than 120 countries, primarily to the, Japan, Southeast Asia, SAARC countries, the European Union and the United States.

Overview

As per the 2014 FAO world agriculture statistics India is the world's largest producer of many fresh fruits like banana, mango, guava, papaya, lemon and vegetables like chickpea, okra and milk, major spices like chili, pepper, ginger, fibrous crops such as jute, staples such as millets and castor oil seed. India is the second largest producer of wheat and rice, the world's major food staples.

India is currently the world's second largest producer of several dry fruits, agriculture-based textile raw material, roots and tuber crops, pulses, farmed fish, eggs, coconut, sugarcane and numerous vegetables. India is ranked under the world's five largest producers of over 80% of agricultural produce items, including many cash crops such as coffee and cotton, in 2010. India is one of the world's five largest producers of livestock and poultry meat, with one of the fastest growth rates, as of 2011.

One report from 2008 claimed that India's population is growing faster than its ability to produce rice and wheat. While other recent studies claim that India can easily feed its growing population, plus produce wheat and rice for global exports, if it can reduce food staple spoilage/wastage, improve its infrastructure and raise its farm productivity like those achieved by other developing countries such as Brazil and China.

In fiscal year ending June 2011, with a normal monsoon season, Indian agriculture accomplished an all-time record production of 85.9 million tonnes of wheat, a 6.4% increase from a year earlier. Rice output in India hit a new record at 95.3 million tonnes, a 7% increase from the year earlier. Lentils and many other food staples production also increased year over year. Indian farmers, thus produced about 71 kilograms of wheat and 80 kilograms of rice for every member of Indian population in 2011. The per capita supply of rice every year in India is now higher than the per capita consumption of rice every year in Japan.

India exported $39 billion worth of agricultural products in 2013, making it the seventh largest agricultural exporter worldwide, and the sixth largest net exporter. This represents explosive growth, as in 2004 net exports were about $5 billion. India is the fastest growing exporter of agricultural products over a 10-year period, its $39 billion of net export is more than double the combined exports of the European Union (EU-28). It has become one of the world's largest supplier of rice, cotton, sugar and wheat. India exported around 2 million metric tonnes of wheat and 2.1 million metric tonnes of rice in 2011 to Africa, Nepal, Bangladesh and other regions around the world.

Aquaculture and catch fishery is amongst the fastest growing industries in India. Between 1990 and 2010, the Indian fish capture harvest doubled, while aquaculture harvest tripled. In 2008, India was the world's sixth largest producer of marine and freshwater capture fisheries and the second largest aquaculture farmed fish producer. India exported 600,000 metric tonnes of fish products to nearly half of the world's countries. Though the available nutritional standard is 100% of the requirement, India lags far behind in terms of quality protein intake at 20% which is to be tackled by making available protein rich food products such as eggs, meat, fish, chicken etc. at affordable prices.

India has shown a steady average nationwide annual increase in the kilograms produced per hectare for some agricultural items, over the last 60 years. These gains have come mainly from India's Green Revolution, improving road and power generation infrastructure, knowledge of gains and reforms. Despite these recent accomplishments, agriculture has the potential for major productivity and total output gains, because crop yields in India are still just 30% to 60% of the best sustainable crop yields achievable in the farms of developed and other developing countries. Additionally, post-harvest losses due to poor infrastructure and unorganised retail, caused India to experience some of the highest food losses in the world.

History

Vedic literature provides some of the earliest written record of agriculture in India. Rigveda hymns, for example, describes plowing, fallowing, irrigation, fruit and vegetable cultivation. Other historical evidence suggests rice and cotton were cultivated in the Indus Valley, and plowing patterns from the Bronze Age have been excavated at Kalibangan in Rajasthan. Bhumivargaha, an Indian Sanskrit text, suggested to be 2500 years old, classifies agricultural land into 12 categories: urvara (fertile), ushara (barren), maru (desert), aprahata (fallow), shadvala (grassy), pankikala (muddy), jalaprayah (watery), kachchaha (contiguous to water), sharkara (full of pebbles and pieces of limestone), sharkaravati (sandy), nadimatruka (watered from a river), and devamatruka (rain fed). Some archaeologists believe that rice was a domesticated crop along the banks of the river Ganges in the sixth millennium BC. So were species of winter cereals (barley, oats, and wheat) and legumes (lentil and chickpea) grown in northwest India before the sixth millennium BC. Other crops cultivated in India 3000 to 6000 years ago, include sesame, linseed, safflower, mustard, castor, mung bean, black gram, horse gram, pigeon pea, field pea, grass pea (khesari), fenugreek, cotton, jujube, grapes, dates, jack fruit, mango, mulberry, and black plum]. Indians might have domesticated buffalo (the river type) 5000 years ago.

According to some scientists agriculture was widespread in the Indian peninsula, 10000–3000 years ago, well beyond the fertile plains of the north. For example, one study reports 12 sites in the southern Indian states of [Tamil Nadu], [Andhra Pradesh] and [Karnataka] providing clear evidence of agriculture of pulses [Vigna radiata] and [Macrotyloma uniflorum], millet-grasses (Brachiaria ramosa and Setaria verticillata), wheats (Triticum dicoccum, Triticum durum/ aestivum), barley (Hordeum vulgare), hyacinth bean (Lablab purpureus), pearl millet (Pennisetum glaucum), finger millet (Eleusine coracana), cotton (Gossypium sp.), linseed (Linum sp.), as well as gathered fruits of Ziziphus and two Cucurbitaceae.

Some claim Indian agriculture began by 9000 BC as a result of early cultivation of plants, and domestication of crops and animals. Settled life soon followed with implements and techniques being developed for agriculture. Double monsoons led to two harvests being reaped in one year. Indian products soon reached trading networks and foreign crops were introduced. Plants and animals—considered essential to survival by the Indians—came to be worshipped and venerated.

The middle ages saw irrigation channels reach a new level of sophistication, and Indian crops affected the economies of other regions of the world under Islamic patronage. Land and water management systems were developed with an aim of providing uniform growth.

Despite some stagnation during the later modern era the independent Republic of India was able to develop a comprehensive agricultural programme.

Agriculture and colonialism over 2500 years ago, Indian farmers had discovered and begun farming many spices and sugarcane. It was in India, between the sixth and four BC, that the Persians, followed by the Greeks, discovered the famous "reeds that produce honey without bees" being grown. These were locally called साखर, (Sākhara). On their return journey, the Macedonian soldiers carried the "honey bearing reeds," thus spreading sugar and sugarcane agriculture. People in India had invented, by about 500 BC, the process to produce sugar crystals. In the local language, these crystals were called *khanda* (खण्ड), which is the source of the word *candy*.

Before the 18th century, cultivation of sugarcane was largely confined to India. A few merchants began to trade in sugar – a luxury and an expensive spice in Europe until the 18th century. Sugar became widely popular in 18th-century Europe, then graduated to become a human necessity in the 19th century all over the world. This evolution of taste and demand for sugar as an essential food ingredient unleashed major economic and social changes. Sugarcane does not grow in cold, frost-prone climate; therefore, tropical and semitropical colonies were sought. Sugarcane plantations, just like cotton farms, became a major driver of large and forced human migrations in the 19th century and early 20th century – of people from Africa and from India, both in millions – influencing the ethnic mix, political conflicts and cultural evolution of Caribbean, South American, Indian Ocean and Pacific Island nations.

The history and past accomplishments of Indian agriculture thus influenced, in part, colonialism, slavery and slavery-like indentured labour practices in the New World, Caribbean wars and world history in 18th and 19th centuries.

Indian agriculture after independence

Green Revolution

The Green Revolution in India started in 1965. It was founded by M. S. Swaminathan. The Bengal famine of 1943 under the British rule was one of the most severe famines that killed over 3 million people. There was no help from the industrial sector, so the agricultural sector during the British rule was a disaster for the people of India. Shortly after independence from the British in 1947 India realised that there was a need to become self-sufficient. This ushered in India's Green Revolution. It began with the decision to adopt superior yielding using disease resistant wheat varieties in combination with better farming knowledge to improve productivity. The major parties involved in executing the plan were the Government of India, multilateral and bilateral donors, International Agricultural Research Institution, farmers, and peasants.

The Green Revolution in India marked a period of time when agricultural practices shifted from traditional practices to more technological methods. Traditional farming included better irrigation systems, mixed cropping and the planting of local species. Technological approaches have given rise to input intensive and unsustainable agricultural practices that ultimately reduce the ground water table, causing erosion and loss in biodiversity. As part of this shift, farmers shifted from using wheel-barrows and bullock carts to mechanised vehicles.

The Green Revolution focused on the introduction and growth of high yielding varieties (HYVs) of plants and grains. This practice spread across various states in India such as Punjab, Haryana, Western Uttar Pradesh, Tamil Nadu and Kerala. This shift in agricultural technique has caused and continues to cause irreversible changes including deterioration in soil health and nutrients. This practice makes it difficult to shift back to organic farming on the same land.

The state of Punjab led India's Green Revolution and earned the distinction of being the country's bread basket. The initial increase in production was centered on the irrigated areas of the states of Punjab, Haryana and western Uttar Pradesh. With the farmers and the government officials focusing on farm productivity and knowledge transfer, India's total food grain production soared. A hectare of Indian wheat farm that produced an average of 0.8 tonnes in 1948, produced 4.7 tonnes of wheat in 1975 from the same land. Such rapid growth in farm productivity enabled India to become self-sufficient by the 1970s. It also empowered the smallholder farmers to seek further means to increase food staples produced per hectare. By 2000, Indian farms were adopting wheat varieties capable of yielding 6 tonnes of wheat per hectare.

There have been various discrepancies regarding crop yield since the start of the Green Revolution. Proponents of the Green Revolution say that it solved the problem of malnutrition but adversaries say that it made it worse. One of the reasons is because monoculture and chemical fertilisers have taken the nutrition out of the food and the soil. There have been many myths regarding soil, high yielding varieties (HYV) [133] and industrial breeding in comparison to organic breeding of plants. The myth of the HYVs - they produce a high partial yield, low total system yield, indigenous varieties get a better yield than the HYVs. Industrial breeding focuses on quantity rather than nutrition per acre, partial yield rather than multiple crops, this type of breeding and planting also removes the focus from local varieties of plants and shifts it to plants that are traded worldwide.

Post-independence agriculture

In the years since its independence, India has made immense progress towards food security. Indian population has tripled, and food-grain production more than quadrupled. There has been a substantial increase in available food-grain per capita.

The state of Punjab led India's Green Revolution and earned the distinction of being the country's bread basket.

Before the mid-1960s India relied on imports and food aid to meet domestic requirements. However, two years of severe drought in 1965 and 1966 convinced India to reform its agricultural policy and that they could not rely on foreign aid and imports for food security. India adopted significant policy reforms focused on the goal of food grain self-sufficiency. This ushered in India's Green Revolution. It began with the decision to adopt superior yielding, disease resistant wheat varieties in combination with better farming knowledge to improve productivity. The state of Punjab led India's Green Revolution and earned the distinction of being the country's bread basket.

The initial increase in production was centred on the irrigated areas of the states of Punjab, Haryana and western Uttar Pradesh. With the farmers and the government officials focusing on farm productivity and knowledge transfer, India's total food grain production soared. A hectare of Indian wheat farm that produced an average of 0.8 tonnes in 1948, produced 4.7 tonnes of wheat in 1975 from the same land. Such rapid growth in farm productivity enabled India to become self-sufficient by the 1970s. It also empowered the smallholder farmers to seek further means to increase food staples produced per hectare. By 2000, Indian farms were adopting wheat varieties capable of yielding 6 tonnes of wheat per hectare.

With agricultural policy success in wheat, India's Green Revolution technology spread to rice. However, since irrigation infrastructure was very poor, Indian farmers innovated with tube-wells, to harvest ground water. When gains from the new technology reached their limits in the states of initial adoption, the technology spread in the 1970s and 1980s to the states of eastern India – Bihar, Odisha and West Bengal. The lasting benefits of the improved seeds and new technology extended principally to the irrigated areas which account for about one-third of the harvested crop area. In the 1980s, Indian agriculture policy shifted to "evolution of a production pattern in line with the demand pattern" leading to a shift in emphasis to other agricultural commodities like oil seed, fruit and vegetables. Farmers began adopting improved methods and technologies in dairying, fisheries and livestock, and meeting the diversified food needs of a growing population.

As with rice, the lasting benefits of improved seeds and improved farming technologies now largely depends on whether India develops infrastructure such as irrigation network, flood control systems, reliable electricity production capacity, all-season rural and urban highways, cold storage to prevent spoilage, modern retail, and competitive buyers of produce from Indian farmers. This is increasingly the focus of Indian agriculture policy.

India ranks 74 out of 113 major countries in terms of food security index. India's agricultural economy is undergoing structural changes. Between 1970 and 2011, the GDP share of agriculture has fallen from 43% to 16%. This isn't because of reduced importance of agriculture or a consequence of agricultural policy. This is largely because of the rapid economic growth in services, industrial output, and non-agricultural sectors in India between 2000 and 2010.

Agricultural scientist MS Swaminathan has played a vital role in the green revolution. In 2013, NDTV awarded him as 25 living legend of India for outstanding contribution to agriculture and making India a food sovereign country.

Irrigation

Indian irrigation infrastructure includes a network of major and minor canals from rivers, groundwater well-based systems, tanks, and other rainwater harvesting projects for agricultural activities. Of these, the groundwater system is the largest. Of the 160 million hectares of cultivated land in India, about 39 million hectare can be irrigated by groundwater wells and an additional 22 million hectares by irrigation canals. In 2010, only about 35% of agricultural land in India was reliably irrigated. About 2/3rd cultivated land in India is dependent on monsoons. The improvements in irrigation infrastructure in the last 50 years have helped India improve food security, reduce dependence on monsoons, improve agricultural productivity and create rural job opportunities. Dams used for irrigation projects have helped provide drinking water to a growing rural population, control flood and prevent drought-related damage to agriculture. However, free electricity and attractive minimum support price for water intensive crops such as sugarcane and rice have encouraged ground water mining leading to groundwater depletion and poor water quality. A news report in 2019 states that more than 60% of the water available for farming in India is consumed by rice and sugar, two crops that occupy 24% of the cultivable area.

Output

As of 2011, India had a large and diverse agricultural sector, accounting, on average, for about 16% of GDP and 10% of export earnings. India's arable land area of 159.7 million hectares (394.6 million acres) is the second largest in the world, after the United States. Its gross irrigated crop area of 82.6 million hectares (215.6 million acres) is the largest in the world. India is among the top three global producers of many crops, including wheat, rice, pulses, cotton, peanuts, fruits and vegetables. Worldwide, as of 2011, India had the largest herds of buffalo and cattle, is the largest producer of milk and has one of the largest and fastest growing poultry industries.

Major products and yields

The following table presents the 20 most important agricultural products in India, by economic value, in 2009. Included in the table is the average productivity of India's farms for each produce. For context and comparison, included is the average of the most productive farms in the world and name of country where the most productive farms existed in 2010. The table suggests India has large potential for further accomplishments from productivity increases, in increased agricultural output and agricultural incomes.

Largest agricultural products in India by value[71][72]

Rank	*Commodity*	*Value (US$, 2016)*	*Unit price (US$ / kilogram, 2009)*	*Average yield (tonnes per hectare, 2017)*	*Most productive country (tonnes per hectare, 2017)*	
1.	Rice	$70.18 billion	0.27	3.85	9.82	Australia
2.	Buffalo milk	$43.09 billion	0.4	2.00	2.00	India
3.	Cow milk	$32.55 billion	0.31	1.2	10.3	Israel
4.	Wheat	$26.06 billion	0.15	2.8	8.9	Netherlands

(*Contd...*)

5.	Cotton (lint & seeds)	$23.30 billion	1.43	1.6	4.6	Israel
6.	Mangoes, guavas	$14.52 billion	0.6	6.3	40.6	Cape Verde
7.	Fresh vegetables	$11.87 billion	0.19	13.4	76.8	United States
8.	Chicken meat	$9.32 billion	0.64	10.6	20.2	Cyprus
9.	Potatoes	$8.23 billion	0.15	19.9	44.3	United States
10.	Banana	$8.13 billion	0.28	37.8	59.3	Indonesia
11.	Sugar cane	$7.44 billion	0.03	66	125	Peru
12.	Maize	$5.81 billion	0.42	1.1	5.5	Nicaragua
13.	Oranges	$5.62 billion				
14.	Tomatoes	$5.50 billion	0.37	19.3	55.9	China
15.	Chick peas	$5.40 billion	0.4	0.9	2.8	China
16.	Okra	$5.25 billion	0.35	7.6	23.9	Israel
17.	Soybeans	$5.13 billion	0.26	1.1	3.7	Turkey
18.	Hen eggs	$4.64 billion	2.7	0.1	0.42	Japan
19.	Cauliflower and broccoli	$4.33 billion	2.69	0.138	0.424	Thailand
20.	Onions	$4.05 billion	0.21	16.6	67.3	Ireland

The Statistics Office of the Food and Agriculture Organisation reported that, per final numbers for 2009, India had grown to become the world's largest producer of the following agricultural products:

- Fresh fruit
- Lemons and limes
- Buffalo milk, whole, fresh
- Castor oil seeds
- Sunflower seeds
- Sorghum
- Millet
- Spices
- Okra
- Jute
- Beeswax
- Bananas
- Mangoes, mangosteens, guavas
- Pulses
- Indigenous buffalo meat
- Fruit, tropical
- Ginger
- Chick peas

- Areca nuts
- Other bastfibres
- Pigeon peas
- Papayas
- Chillies and peppers, dry
- Anise, badian, fennel, coriander
- Goat milk, whole, fresh

Per final numbers for 2009, India is the world's second largest producer of the following agricultural products:

- Wheat
- Rice
- Fresh vegetables
- Sugar cane
- Groundnuts, with shell
- Lentils
- Garlic
- Cauliflowers and broccoli
- Peas, green
- Sesame seed
- Cashew nuts, with shell
- Silk-worm cocoons, reelable
- Cow milk, whole, fresh
- Tea
- Potatoes
- Onions
- Cotton lint
- Cotton seed
- Eggplants (aubergines)
- Nutmeg, mace and cardamoms
- Indigenous goat meat
- Cabbages and other brassicas
- Pumpkins, squash and gourds

In 2009, India was the world's third largest producer of eggs, oranges, coconuts, tomatoes, peas and beans.

In addition to growth in total output, agriculture in India has shown an increase in average agricultural output per hectare in last 60 years. The table below presents average farm productivity in India over three farming years for some crops. Improving road and power generation infrastructure, knowledge gains and reforms has allowed India to increase farm productivity between 40% to 500% over 40 years. India's recent accomplishments in crop yields while being impressive, are still just 30% to 60% of the best crop yields achievable in the farms of developed as well as other developing countries. Additionally, despite these gains in farm productivity, losses after harvest due to poor infrastructure and unorganised retail cause India to experience some of the highest food losses in the world.

Agriculture productivity in India, growth in average yields from 1970 to 2010

Crop	*Average YIELD, 1970–1971*	*Average YIELD, 1990–1991*	*Average YIELD, 2010–2011*
	kilogram per hectare	kilogram per hectare	kilogram per hectare
Rice	1123	1740	2240
Wheat	1307	2281	2938
Pulses	524	578	689
Oilseeds	579	771	1325
Sugarcane	48322	65395	68596
Tea	1182	1652	1669
Cotton	106	225	510

India and China are competing to establish the world record on rice yields. Yuan Longping of China National Hybrid Rice Research and Development Centre set a world record for rice yield in 2010 at 19 tonnes per hectare in a demonstration plot. In 2011, this record was surpassed by an Indian farmer, Sumant Kumar, with 22.4 tonnes per hectare in Bihar, also in a demonstration plot. These farmers claim to have employed newly developed rice breeds and system of rice intensification (SRI), a recent innovation in farming. The claimed Chinese and Indian yields have yet to be demonstrated on 7 hectare farm lots and that these are reproducible over two consecutive years on the same farm.

Horticulture

The total production and economic value of horticultural produce, such as fruits, vegetables and nuts has doubled in India over the 10-year period from 2002 to 2012. In 2012, the production from horticulture exceeded grain output for the first time. The total horticulture produce reached 277.4 million metric tonnes in 2013, making India the second largest producer of horticultural products after China. Of this, India in 2013 produced 81 million tonnes of fruits, 162 million tonnes of vegetables, 5.7 million tonnes of spices, 17 million tonnes of nuts and plantation products (cashew, cacao, coconut, etc.), 1 million tonnes of aromatic horticulture produce and 1.7 million tonnes of flowers (7.6 billion cut flowers).

Horticultural productivity in India, 2013

Country	*Area under fruits production (million hectares)*	*Average Fruits Yield (Metric tonnes per hectare*	*Area under vegetable production (million hectares)*	*Average Vegetable Yield (Metric tonnes per hectare)*
India	7.0	11.6	9.2	52.36
China	11.8	11.6	24.6	23.4
Spain	1.54	9.1	0.32	39.3
United States	1.14	23.3	1.1	32.5
World	57.3	11.3	60.0	19.7

During the 2013 fiscal year, India exported horticulture products worth ₹ 144 billion (US$2.0 billion), nearly double the value of its 2010 exports. Along with these farm-level gains, the losses between farm and consumer increased and are estimated to range between 51 and 82 million metric tonnes a year.

Organic agriculture

Organic agriculture has fed India for centuries and it is again a growing sector in India. Organic production offers clean and green production methods without the use of synthetic fertilisers and pesticides and it achieves a premium price in the market place. India has 650,000 organic producers, which is more than any other country. India also has 4 million hectares of land certified as organic wild culture, which is third in the world (after Finland and Zambia). As non-availability of edible biomass is impeding the growth of animal husbandry in India, organic production of protein rich cattle, fish and poultry feed using biogas /methane/natural gas by cultivating Methylococcus capsulatus bacteria with tiny land and water footprint is a solution for ensuring adequate protein rich food to the population.

Agriculture based cooperatives

India has seen a huge growth in cooperative societies, mainly in the farming sector, since 1947 when the country gained independence from Britain. The country has networks of cooperatives at the local, regional, state and national levels that assist in agricultural marketing. The commodities that are mostly handled are food grains, jute, cotton, sugar, milk, fruit and nuts. Support by the state government led to more than 25,000 cooperatives being set up by the 1990s in the state of Maharashtra.

Sugar industry

Most of the sugar production in India takes place at mills owned by local cooperative societies. The members of the society include all farmers, small and large, supplying sugarcane to the mill. Over the last fifty years, the local sugar mills have played a crucial part in encouraging political participation and as a stepping stone for aspiring politicians. This is particularly true in the state of Maharashtra where a large number of politicians belonging to the Congress party or NCP had ties to sugar cooperatives from their local area and has created a symbiotic relationship between the sugar factories and local politics. However, the policy of "profits for the company but losses to be borne by the government", has made a number of these operations inefficient.

Marketing

As with sugar, cooperatives play a significant part in the overall marketing of fruit and vegetables in India. Since the 1980s, the amount of produce handled by Cooperative Societies has increased exponentially. Common fruit and vegetables marketed by the societies include bananas, mangoes, grapes, onions and many others.

Dairy industry

Dairy farming based on the Amul Pattern, with a single marketing cooperative, is India's largest self-sustaining industry and its largest rural employment provider. Successful implementation of the Amul model has made India the world's largest milk producer. Here small, marginal farmers with a couple or so heads of milk cattle queue up twice daily to pour milk from their small containers into the village union collection points. The milk after processing at the district unions is then marketed by the state cooperative federation nationally under the Amul brand name, India's largest food brand. With the Anand pattern three-fourths of the price paid by the mainly urban consumers goes into the hands of millions of small dairy farmers, who are the owners of the brand and the cooperative.

Banking and rural credit

Cooperative banks play a great part in providing credit in rural parts of India. Just like the sugar cooperatives, these institutions serve as the power base for local politicians.

Problems

India lacks cold storage, food packaging as well as safe and efficient rural transport system. This causes one of the world's highest food spoilage rates, particularly during monsoons and other adverse weather conditions. Food travels to the Indian consumer through a slow and inefficient chain of traders. Consumers buy agricultural produce in suburban markets known as such as one shown or from roadside vendors.

Indian agriculture includes a mix of traditional to modern farming techniques. In some parts of India, traditional use of cattle to plough remains in use. Traditional farms have some of the lowest per capita productivities and farmer incomes.

Since 2002, India has become the world's largest manufacturer of tractors with 29% of world's output in 2013; it is also the world's largest tractor market.

"Slow agricultural growth is a concern for policymakers as some two-thirds of India's people depend on rural employment for a living. Current agricultural practices are neither economically nor environmentally sustainable and India's yields for many agricultural commodities are low. Poorly maintained irrigation systems and almost universal lack of good extension services are among the factors responsible. Farmers' access to markets is hampered by poor roads, rudimentary market infrastructure, and excessive regulation."

— *World Bank: "India Country Overview 2008"*

"With a population of just over 1.3 billion, India is the world's largest democracy. In the past decade, the country has witnessed accelerated economic growth, emerged as a global player with the world's fourth largest economy in purchasing power parity terms, and made progress towards achieving most of the Millennium Development Goals. India's integration into the global economy has been accompanied by impressive economic growth that has brought significant economic and social benefits to the country. Nevertheless, disparities in income and human development are on the rise. Preliminary estimates suggest that in 2009–10 the combined all India poverty rate was 32 % compared to 37 % in 2004–05. Going forward, it will be essential for India to build a productive, competitive, and diversified agricultural sector and facilitate rural, non-farm entrepreneurship and employment. Encouraging policies that promote competition in agricultural marketing will ensure that farmers receive better prices."

— *World Bank: "India Country Overview 2011"*

A 2003 analysis of India's agricultural growth from 1970 to 2001 by the Food and Agriculture Organisation identified systemic problems in Indian agriculture. For food staples, the annual growth rate in production during the six-year segments 1970–76, 1976–82, 1982–88, 1988–1994, 1994–2000 were found to be respectively 2.5, 2.5, 3.0, 2.6, and 1.8% per annum. Corresponding analyses for the index of total agricultural production show a similar pattern, with the growth rate for 1994–2000 attaining only 1.5% per annum.

The biggest problem of farmers is the low price for their farm produce. A recent study showed that proper pricing based on energy of production and equating farming wages to Industrial wages may be beneficial for the farmers.

Impact of climate change

India plays a large role in global food security. India produced 148.8 million tons of rice and 78.6 million tons of wheat in 2008. Climate change has reduced this number since 1980 through. The effect of climate change on the Indian agriculture is a combination of the long lived global emissions of greenhouse gases (LLGHGs) and short lived climate pollutants (SLCPs) among precipitation and black carbon. Wheat and rice yield dropped from 1980-2010 by over 36% and 20% respectively in Uttar Pradesh and Uttarachal. There was a reduction in wheat production of 3.5% throughout India. The impacts of climate change on agriculture in India would not only affect the practices of agriculture and the country's economy but will also have major socio-economic implications as 56% of employment is under the agricultural sector.

Infrastructure

India has very poor rural roads affecting timely supply of inputs and timely transfer of outputs from Indian farms. Irrigation systems are inadequate, leading to crop failures in some parts of the country because of lack of water. In other areas regional floods, poor seed quality and inefficient farming practices, lack of cold storage and harvest spoilage cause over 30% of farmer's produce going to waste, lack of organised retail and competing buyers thereby limiting Indian farmer's ability to sell the surplus and commercial crops.

The Indian farmer receives just 10% to 23% of the price the Indian consumer pays for exactly the same produce, the difference going to losses, inefficiencies and middlemen. Farmers in developed economies of Europe and the United States receive 64% to 81%.

Productivity

Although India has attained self-sufficiency in food staples, the productivity of its farms is below that of Brazil, the United States, France and other nations. Indian wheat farms, for example, produce about a third of the wheat per hectare per year compared to farms in France. Rice productivity in India was less than half that of China. Other staples productivity in India is similarly low. Indian total factor productivity growth remains below 2% per annum; in contrast, China's total factor productivity growths is about 6% per annum, even though China also has smallholding farmers. Several studies suggest India could eradicate its hunger and malnutrition and be a major source of food for the world by achieving productivity comparable with other countries.

By contrast, Indian farms in some regions post the best yields, for sugarcane, cassava and tea crops.

Crop yields vary significantly between Indian states. Some states produce two to three times more grain per acre than others.

As the map shows, the traditional regions of high agricultural productivity in India are the North West (Punjab, Haryana and Western Uttar Pradesh), coastal districts on both coasts, West Bengal and Tamil Nadu. In recent years, the states of Madhya Pradesh, Jharkhand, and Chhattisgarh in central India and Gujarat in the west have shown rapid agricultural growth.

The table compares the statewide average yields for a few major agricultural crops in India, for 2001–2002.

Crop	***Average farm yield in Bihar***	***Average farm yield in Karnataka***	***Average farm yield in Punjab***
	kilogram per hectare	kilogram per hectare	kilogram per hectare
Wheat	2020	Unknown	3880
Rice	1370	2380	3130
Pulses	610	470	820
Oil seeds	620	680	1200
Sugarcane	45510	79560	65300

Crop yields for some farms in India are within 90% of the best achieved yields by farms in developed countries such as the United States and in European Union. No single state of India is best in every crop. Tamil Nadu achieved highest yields in rice and sugarcane, Haryana in wheat and coarse grains, Karnataka in cotton, Bihar in pulses, while other states do well in horticulture, aquaculture, flower and fruit plantations. These differences in agricultural productivity are a function of local infrastructure, soil quality, micro-climates, local resources, farmer knowledge and innovations.

The Indian food distribution system is highly inefficient. Movement of agricultural produce is heavily regulated, with inter-state and even inter-district restrictions on marketing and movement of agricultural goods.

One study suggests Indian agricultural policy should best focus on improving rural infrastructure primarily in the form of irrigation and flood control infrastructure, knowledge transfer of better yielding and more disease resistant seeds. Additionally, cold storage, hygienic food packaging and efficient modern retail to reduce waste can improve output and rural incomes.

The low productivity in India is a result of the following factors:

- The average size of land holdings is very small (less than 2 hectares) and is subject to fragmentation due to land ceiling acts, and in some cases, family disputes. Such small holdings are often over-manned, resulting in disguised unemployment and low productivity of labour. Some reports claim smallholder farming may not because of poor productivity, since the productivity is higher in China and many developing economies even though China smallholder farmers constitute over 97% of its farming population. A Chinese smallholder farmer is able to rent his land to larger farmers, China's organised retail and extensive Chinese highways are able to provide the incentive and infrastructure necessary to its farmers for sharp increases in farm productivity.
- Adoption of modern agricultural practices and use of technology is inadequate in comparison with Green Revolution methods and technologies, hampered by ignorance of such practices, high costs and impracticality in the case of small land holdings.
- According to the World Bank, Indian branch's Priorities for Agriculture and Rural Development, India's large agricultural subsidies are hampering productivity-enhancing investment. This evaluation is based largely on a productivity agenda and does not take any ecological implications into account. According to a neo-liberal view, over-regulation of agriculture has increased costs, price risks and uncertainty because the government intervenes in labour, land, and credit markets. India has inadequate infrastructure and services. The World Bank also says that the allocation of water is inefficient, unsustainable and inequitable. The irrigation infrastructure is deteriorating. The overuse of water is being covered by over-pumping aquifers but, as these are falling by one foot of groundwater each year, this is a limited resource. The Intergovernmental Panel on Climate Change released a

report that food security may be a big problem in the region post-2030.

- Illiteracy, general socio-economic backwardness, slow progress in implementing land reforms and inadequate or inefficient finance and marketing services for farm produce.
- Inconsistent government policy. Agricultural subsidies and taxes are often changed without notice for short term political ends.
- Irrigation facilities are inadequate, as revealed by the fact that only 52.6% of the land was irrigated in 2003–04, which result in farmers still being dependent on rainfall, specifically the monsoon season. A good monsoon results in a robust growth for the economy, while a poor monsoon leads to a sluggish growth. Farm credit is regulated by NABARD, which is the statutory apex agent for rural development in the subcontinent. At the same time, over-pumping made possible by subsidised electric power is leading to an alarming drop in aquifer levels.
- A third of all food that is produced rots due to inefficient supply chains and the use of the "Walmart model" to improve efficiency is blocked by laws against foreign investment in the retail sector.

Farmer suicides

In 2012, the National Crime Records Bureau of India reported 13,754 farmer suicides. Farmer suicides account for 11.2% of all suicides in India. Most of the farmer suicides were happening in Andhra Pradesh, Maharashtra, Chhattisgarh, Kerala and Karnataka. At the time, financial debt was increasing and showed no signs of reducing. Some of the reasons for debt come from increasing cost of cultivation on farms due to price increase of chemical fertilisers and seeds, more frequent crop failures, water scarcity, unstable income and trade liberalisation. Financial debt is one of many reasons such as monsoon failure, high debt burdens, genetically modified crops, government policies, public mental health, personal issues and family problems.

Diversion of agricultural land for non-agricultural purpose

Indian National Policy for Farmers of 2007 stated that "prime farmland must be conserved for agriculture except under exceptional circumstances, provided that the agencies that are provided with agricultural land for non-agricultural projects should compensate for treatment and full development of equivalent degraded or wastelands elsewhere". The policy suggested that, as far as possible, land with low farming yields or that was not farmable should be earmarked for non-agricultural purposes such as construction, industrial parks and other commercial development.

Amartya Sen offered a counter viewpoint, stating that "prohibiting the use of agricultural land for commercial and industrial development is ultimately self-defeating." He stated that agricultural land may be better suited for non-agriculture purposes if industrial production could generate many times more than the value of the product produced by agriculture. Sen suggested India needed to bring productive industry everywhere, wherever there are advantages of production, market needs and the locational preferences of managers, engineers, technical experts as well as unskilled labour because of education, healthcare and other infrastructure. He stated that instead of government controlling land allocation based on soil characteristics, the market economy should determine productive allocation of land.

The required level of investment for the development of marketing, storage and cold storage infrastructure is estimated to be huge. The government has not been able to implement schemes to raise investment in marketing infrastructure. Among these schemes are 'Construction of Rural Go downs', 'Market Research and Information Network', and 'Development / Strengthening of Agricultural Marketing Infrastructure, Grading and Standardisation'.

The Indian Council of Agricultural Research (ICAR), established in 1905, was responsible for the search leading to the < Indian Green Revolution > of the 1970s. The ICAR is the apex body in agriculture and related allied fields, including research and education. The Union Minister of Agriculture is the president of the ICAR. The Indian Agricultural Statistics Research Institute develops new techniques for the design of agricultural experiments, analyses data in agriculture, and specialises in statistical techniques for animal and plant breeding.

Recently (May 2016) the Government of India has set up the Farmers Commission to completely evaluate the agriculture programme. Its recommendations have had a mixed reception.

In November 2011, India announced major reforms in organised sector. These reforms would include logistics and retail of agricultural produce. The announcement led to major political controversy. The reforms were placed on hold by the government in December 2011.

In the summer of 2012, the subsidised electricity for pumping, which has caused an alarming drop in aquifer levels, put additional strain on the country's electrical grid due to a 19% drop in monsoon rains and may have contributed to a blackout across much of the country. In response the state of Bihar offered farmers over $100 million in subsidised diesel to operate their pumps.

In 2015, Prime Minister Narendra Modi announced to double farmer's income by 2022.

Startups with niche technology and new business models are working to solve problems in Indian agriculture and its marketing. Kandawale is one of such e-commerce website which sells Indian red onions to bulk users direct from farmers, reducing unnecessary cost escalations.

Chapter - 4

Public Sector Undertakings in India

Main base of the Five Year Plans was to set up the large Public Sector companies entirely owned by the Central or State Government. In constructing large scale industries, it is required to find out what PSU should construct. It takes huge capital fund to construct any Public Sector Unit.

Government of India introduced the Planning Commission in 1951 and first five year plan was formulated and implemented during 1951-56. Under this Plan, the agriculture was given the first priority and 40% of the planning expenditure was allocated to the agriculture.

In Second Five Year Plan and thereafter, the priority was given to erecting large public sector industries. When such plans are designed, it is necessary to carefully set up such industries. Land needs to be identified for such project. Then the cost of the land needs to be paid. Big building construction is necessary to set up the heavy capital goods productive machinery in the premises. These machinery needs to be selected from various countries on the multi-purpose use of such machines. Then the machine which is the most favourable for our purpose needs to be selected. There will be negotiation on terms of purchasing machine with the technical team coming to India to train the Indian Engineers how to operate the machinery from all angles. Price of the machine and schedule of payments are required to be finalised. Sources of raising funds for payments need to be observed and finalised. Generally such machines are manufactured in foreign countries like USA, German, England etc. The payments of machinery and technical knowhow needs to be paid in USD currency. We have to raise USD from IMF or World Bank on the terms most suitable for us. These funds needs to be repaid on times to avoid bail-out and other critical financial situation. Planning for this needs to be meticulously done and implemented.

Machinery will be brought and set up in such a way that it gives optimum production. For this purpose, the foreign technical team will study the production process and the machinery will be set up accordingly. There may be deficit financing during the initial stage until the PSU gives normal and full optimum production. Break-even needs to be worked out and meticulously implemented. Foreign Company's Engineers should train our engineers and the worker fully and make them skilled Engineers and skilled workers. Raw materials should be stocked in ample quality and workers' need to be taken into account. Work atmosphere should be pleasant. There should proper transport system for workers to bring workers from home and return them to their residential places after working hours. Residential quarters need to be constructed near the work factory and there should schools and colleges to educate the workers' children and their families. Healthy food needs to be provided to workers to increase their work efficiency and the workers should be treated nicely by their superiors by understanding their difficulties and meeting them on time. Trade Union will do this part effectively by negotiation with the Human Resources personnel in the Factory. Workers should be paid good salary to meet their family's financial requirements. All these factors will pay good dividends and the production will be optimum.

Hospitals should be built up and expert doctors on all fields should be appointed to give standard medical treatment to workers and their family members in normal circumstances and during epidemics like Corona virus. Medical expenses should be paid from the employees medical insurance for workers and their families or special medical donation by the concerned company. Medical treatment should b free of cost for the workers and their family members.

Burden of repaying borrowed foreign exchange loan should be entirely borne by the Central Government and should not be shifted to PSU. PSU should commence the capital goods production at optimum level as per the schedule time so that there will be no deficit financing issue or bail-out package for regular servicing the external debt.

A state-owned enterprise in India is called a public sector undertaking (PSU) or a public sector enterprise. Those companies that are owned by the union government of India or one of the many state or territorial governments or both. The company stock needs to be majority-owned by the government to be a PSU. PSUs strictly may be classified as central public sector enterprises (CPSUs, CPSEs) or state level public enterprises (SLPEs). In 1951, there were just five enterprises in the public sector in India, but in March 2019 this had increased to 348. These enterprises represents total investment of RS. 16,40,628 crores as on 31st March, 2019. Total paid up capital as on 31 March, 2019 stands at 2,75,697 crores. CPSE's have earned revenue of 25,43,370 crores during financial year 2018-19. They are administered by the Ministry of Heavy Industries and Public Enterprises.

History

When India achieved independence in 1947, it was primarily an agricultural country with a weak industrial base. There were only eighteen Indian Ordinance Factories in the country which the British had established for their own economic interest and rule the subcontinent with brutal force. The national consensus was in favour of rapid industrialisation of the economy which was seen as the key to economic development, improving living standards and economic sovereignty. Building upon the Bombay Plan, which noted the requirement of government intervention and regulation, the first Industrial Policy Resolution announced in 1948 laid down broad contours of the strategy of industrial development. Subsequently, the Planning Commission was formed by a cabinet resolution in March 1950 and the Industrial (Development and Regulation) Act was enacted in 1951 with the objective of empowering the government to take necessary steps to regulate industrial development. Prime Minister Jawaharlal Nehru promoted an economic policy based on import substitution industrialization and advocated a mixed economy. He believed that the establishment of basic and heavy industry was fundamental to the development and modernisation of the Indian economy. India's second five year plan (1956–60) and the Industrial Policy Resolution of 1956 emphasised the development of public sector enterprises to meet Nehru's national industrialisation policy. His vision was carried forward by Dr. V. Krishnamurthy known as the "father, of Public Sector Undertakings in India". Indian statistician Prasanta Chandra Mahalanobis was instrumental to its formulation, which was subsequently termed the Feldman–Mahalanobis model.

The major consideration for the setting up of PSUs, was to accelerate the growth of core sectors of the economy; to serve the equipment needs of strategically important sectors, and to generate employment and income. A large number of "sick units" were taken over from the private sector. Additionally, Indira Gandhi's government nationalised fourteen of India's largest private banks in 1969, and an additional six in 1980. This government-led industrial policy, with corresponding restrictions on private enterprise, was the dominant pattern of Indian economic development until the 1991 Indian economic crisis. After the crisis, the government began disinvesting its ownership of several PSUs to raise capital and privatised companies facing poor financial performance and low efficiency.

Governance

Certain public sector undertakings have been awarded additional financial autonomy. These companies are "public sector companies that have comparative advantages", giving them greater autonomy to compete in the global market so as to "support [them] in their drive to become global giants". Financial autonomy was initially awarded to nine PSUs as *Navratna* status in 1997. Originally, the term *Navratna* meant a talisman composed of nine precious gems. Later, this term was adopted in the courts of Gupta emperor Vikramaditya and Mughal emperor Akbar, as the collective name for nine extraordinary courtiers at their respective courts.

In 2010, the government established the higher *Maharatna* category, which raises a company's investment ceiling from ₹ 1,000 crore to ₹ 5,000 crore. The *Maharatna* firms can now decide on investments of up to 15 percent of their net worth in a project while the *Navaratna* companies could invest up to ₹ 1,000 crore without explicit government approval. Two categories of *Miniratnas* afford less extensive financial autonomy.

Guidelines for awarding *Ratna* status are as follows:

	Maharatna	*Navratna*	*Miniratna Category-I*	*Miniratna Category-II*
Eligibility	Three years with an average annual net profit of over Rs. 2500 crore, OR Average annual Net worth of Rs. 10,000 crore for 3 years, OR Average annual Turnover of	A score of 60 (out of 100), based on six parameters which include net profit, net worth, total manpower cost, total cost of production, cost of services, PBDIT (Profit Before Depreciation,	Have made profits continuously for the last three years or earned a net profit of Rs. 30 crore or more in one of the three years	Have made profits continuously for the last three years and should have a positive net worth.

(*Contd...*)

	Rs. 20,000 crore for 3 years (against Rs 25,000 crore prescribed earlier)	Interest and Taxes), capital employed, etc., AND A company must first be a Miniratna and have 4 independent directors on its board before it can be made a Navratna.		
Benefits for investment	Rs. 1,000 crore - Rs. 5,000 crore, or free to decide on investments up to 15% of their net worth in a project	up to Rs. 1,000 crore or 15% of their net worth on a single project or 30% of their net worth in the whole year (not exceeding Rs. 1,000 crores).	up to Rs. 500 crore or equal to their net worth, whichever is lower.	up to Rs. 300 crore or up to 50% of their net worth, whichever is lower.

PSUs in India are also categorised based on their special non-financial objectives and are registered under Section 8 of Companies Act, 2013 (erstwhile Section 25 of Companies Act, 1956).

Top Profit Making Public Sector Undertakings:

Net Profit for Financial Year 2018-19

Sl. No.	*CPSE Name*	*Net Profit (In cr. INR)*
1.	Oil & Natural Gas Corporation Ltd.(ONGC)	26,716
2.	Indian Oil Corporation Ltd.	16,894
3.	NTPC Ltd.	11,750
4.	Coal India Ltd	10,470
5.	Power Grid Corporation of India Ltd	9,939
6.	Bharat Petroleum Corporation Ltd	7,132
7.	Power Finance Corporation Ltd.	6,953
8.	Mahanadi Coalfields Ltd	6,040
9.	Hindustan Petroleum Corporation Ltd	6,029
10.	Gail (India) Ltd	6,029

Bharat Electronics

Bharat Electronics Limited

भारत इलेक्ट्रॉनिक्स
BHARAT ELECTRONICS

Type: Public Sector Undertaking

Traded as: BSE: 500049

NSE: BEL

Industry:	Aerospace and defence
Founded:	1954 (66 years ago)
Headquarters:	Bengaluru, Karnataka, India
Number of locations:	9 manufacturing units in India
Key people:	M V Gowtama (Chairman & MD)
Products:	Avionics, radars, weapon systems, C4I systems, electronic voting machines, etc.
Revenue:	▲ ₹ 12,921.11 crore (US$1.8 billion) (2020)
Operating income:	▼ ₹ 2,479.17 crore (US$350 million) (2020)
Net income:	▼ ₹ 1,793.83 crore (US$250 million) (2020)
Total assets:	▲ ₹ 20,463.44 crore (US$2.9 billion) (2019)
Total equity:	▲ ₹ 9,018.91 crore (US$1.3 billion) (2019)
Owner:	Government of India (63.17%)
Number of employees:	9,612 (March 2019)
Website:	www.bel-india.in

Bharat Electronics Limited (BEL) is an Indian state-owned aerospace and defence company with about nine factories, and several regional offices in India.

It is owned by the Indian Government and primarily manufactures advanced electronic products for the Indian Armed Forces. BEL is one of nine PSUs under the Ministry of Defence of India. It has been granted *Navratna* status by the Government of India.

History

Bharat Electronics Limited was founded in Bengaluru, Karnataka, India in 1954.

Starting with the manufacture of a few communication equipment in 1956, BEL started producing receiving valves in 1961, germanium semiconductors in 1962 and radio transmitters for AIR in 1964.

- In 1966, BEL set up a radar manufacturing facility for the army and in-house R&D. In 1967, BEL began manufacturing transmitting tubes, silicon devices and integrated circuits. The PCB manufacturing facility was established in 1968.
- In 1970, BEL started making black & white TV picture tubes, X-ray tubes and microwave tubes. In 1971, BEL set up facilities

for the manufacture of integrated circuits and hybrid micro circuits. 1972, BEL established manufacturing facilities for TV transmitters for Doordarshan. In 1973, BEL began manufacturing frigate radars for the navy.

Under the government's policy of decentralisation and due to strategic reasons, BEL set up new units at different location across the country. The second unit of BEL was set up at Ghaziabad in 1974 to manufacture radars and Tropo communication equipment for the Indian Air Force. The third unit was established at Pune in 1979 to manufacture image converter and image intensifier tubes.

- In 1980, the first overseas office of BEL was set up in New York for the procurement of components and materials.
- In 1981, a manufacturing facility for magnesium manganese dioxide batteries was set up at Pune. The Space Electronic Division was set up at Bangaluru to support the satellite programmes in 1982. That year, BEL achieved a turnover of ₹ 1 billion (US$21 million).
- In 1983, the Andhra Scientific Company (ASCO) was taken over by BEL converted it to its fourth manufacturing unit at Machilipatnam.
- In 1985, the fifth unit was set up in Chennai for supply of tank electronics, with proximity to Heavy Vehicles Factory, Chennai of the Ordnance Factory Board. The sixth unit was set up at Panchkula the same year to manufacture military communication equipment.
- In 1986, BEL set up three units. Its seventh unit was set up at Kotdwara to manufacture switching equipment, the eighth unit to manufacture TV glass shell at Taloja (Navi Mumbai) and the ninth unit at Hyderabad to manufacture electronic warfare equipment.
- In 1987, a separate Naval Equipment Division was set up at Bangaluru to give greater focus to naval projects. The first Central Research Laboratory was established at Bangaluru in 1988 to focus on futuristic research and development.
- In 1989, BEL started manufacturing telecom switching and transmission systems and also the set up the Mass Manufacturing Facility in Bangaluru and the manufacture of the first batch of 75,000 electronic voting machines.

The agreement for setting up BEL's first joint venture company, BE DELFT, with M/s Delft of Holland, was signed in 1990. This later became a subsidiary of BEL with the exit of the foreign partner and has been renamed BEL Optronic Devices Limited.

The second Central Research Laboratory was established at Ghaziabad in 1992. The first disinvestment (20%) and listing of the company's shares in the Bangaluru and Mumbai Stock Exchanges took place in same year-1992.

- In 1996, BEL achieved ₹ 10 billion (US$215 million) turnover.
- In 1997, GE BEL, the second joint venture company with M/s GE, USA, was formed as also the third JVC with M/s Multitone, UK, BEL Multitone. The same year, the US imposed supply restrictions on BEL.
- In 1998, BEL set up its second overseas office at Singapore to source components from South East Asia. In the same year US and Europe imposed sanctions on BEL. The company was able to overcome the effects of the sanctions and kept up the promised deliveries to customers.
- In 2000, BEL reorganised its Bangaluru unit into six Strategic Business Units (SBUs). The R&D groups in Bangaluru were also restructured into Specific Core Groups and Product Development Groups. The same year, BEL shares were listed in the National Stock Exchange.
- In 2002, BEL became the first defence PSU to achieve operational Mini Ratna Category I status. In 2003, the company's turnover crossed the ₹ 25 billion mark (US$540 million). In 2005, BEL had a turnover of ₹ 32.20 billion (US$695 million). BEL achieved a turnover of ₹ 35.60 billion (US$767 million) in 2005–06.
- On 12 May 2010, Boeing announced that it received the Data Link II communications technology for the Indian Navy's P-8I from Bharat Electronics Limited (BEL) in April, one month ahead of schedule. BEL delivered the Indian-designed communications system that would enable the exchange of tactical data and messages between Indian Navy aircraft, ships and shore establishments. Boeing installed the system during final assembly of P-8I.

- In 2011, the Indian government-owned Bharat Electronic Limited (BEL) showcased its entire range of C4ISR capabilities including network centric warfare technologies developed in-house at Aero India 2011. These include command and control system, air space management multi sensor tracking, situation simulator and tactical algorithm for air defence applications; battlefield management system and an all-weather 24/7 coastal surveillance system.

In addition, new products and technologies including software defined radios, next generation bulk encrypt or and high data tactical radio were also on show. Airborne products displayed included radar finger printing system, data link, digital flight control computer and identification friend or foe. Also on display were the complete range of optoelectronic equipment, including night vision devices, digital handheld compass and an advanced land navigation system.

BEL is the lead integrator of Akash, the Indian-made guided missile air defence weapon system. Another major system is weapon locating radar, the state-of-the-art passive, phased array radar which has undergone successful user trials by the Indian defence forces.

Products

BEL designs, develops and manufactures a range of products in the following fields:

- Electronic voting machines
- Voter-verified paper audit trail
- Traffic signals
- Radars
    - BEL Weapon Locating Radar
    - BEL Battle Field Surveillance Radar
    - Indian Doppler Radar
    - Samyukta Electronic Warfare System
    - Central Acquisition Radar (3D-CAR)
    - Reporter Radar
- Telecommunications
- Sound and vision broadcasting
- Opto-electronics

- Information technology
- Semiconductors
- Missiles
  - Akash (missile) in partnership with the Ordnance Factory Board
- Sonars
- Composite Communication System (CCS)
- Fire-control system
- Radar
- Electronic warfare systems
- F-INSAS in partnership with the Ordnance Factory Board
- Simulators
- Tank electronics
  - Combined day sight for OFB Arjun MBT
- Defence communications
  - Data Link II communications system for the Indian Navy's P-8I
  - Combat management system for Indian Navy
- Solar systems
- Naval systems
- C4I systems for Air force
- A low-cost tablet PC being used in the Socio-economic Caste Census 2011
- Biometrics Capturing for Nation Population Register
- Encryptors for the Ministry of Home Affairs
- IFF (Identify Friend or Foe) secondary radar
- SDR and IP radio in multiple frequency bands

Some products are manufactured by Bharat Electronics Ltd. with the help of ToT (Transfer of Technology).

Locations

Bharat Electronics Limited has its units in the following cities of India.

- Bangaluru (corporate head office and factory), Karnataka

- Chennai, Tamil Nadu
- Panchkula, Haryana
- Kotdwar, Uttarakhand
- Ghaziabad, Uttar Pradesh
- Pune, Maharashtra
- Hyderabad, Telangana
- Navi Mumbai
- Machilipatnam, Andhra Pradesh

Foreign offices

- New York City
- Singapore
- Hanoi, Vietnam
- Yangon, Myanmar

Regional offices

- New Delhi
- Mumbai
- Kolkata
- Vizag

Subsidiaries

BEL Optronic Devices Ltd

BEL Optronic Devices Ltd. is a subsidiary company of BEL. It was founded in 1990 with the aim of conducting research, development and manufacture of image intensifier tubes and associated high voltage power supply units for use in military, security and commercial systems. The company is headquartered in Pune and earned aggregated revenue of ₹ 516 million (US$7.2 million) during the fiscal year 2007.

Joint ventures

BEL Thales Limited

BEL-Thales Systems Limited is a joint venture company (JVC) between Bharat Electronics Limited and Thales. Incorporated on 28 August

2014, the company is located in the BEL Industrial Estate, Jalahalli, and Bengaluru.

GE-BE Pvt Limited

GE-BE Pvt Limited was set up in 1997 as a joint venture between Bharat Electronics Limited and General Electric Medical System. The facility based at Whitefield, Bangaluru, manufactures X-ray tubes for RAD & F and CT systems, as well as components such as high voltage tanks and detector modules for CT systems. The products are exported worldwide and meet the safety and regulatory standards specified by FDA, CE, MHW, AERB and the facility has been accredited with ISO-9001: ISO-13485 and ISO-14001 certifications. GE-BEL also markets the conventional X-ray tubes made at the Pune unit of BEL. The turnover of GE-BEL during 2004–2005 was over ₹ 4.50 billion (US$97 million) including an export of over ₹ 4.30 billion (US$92 million). The company has been recognised for its outstanding export performance since 1998 by the Export Promotion Councils.

Ownership

As of September 2018, Bharat Electronics Limited is primarily owned by the central government (66%), Mutual Funds and UTI (14%), foreign institutional investors (6%), individual investors (5%) and insurance companies (4%).

Corporate social responsibilities

BEL is involved in various community development initiatives wherever it is present across India. BEL has its own educational institutions among them one is special school for the mentally challenged students. It has set up hospital, crèche and other welfare measures for its employees and their dependents.

BEL assigns some resources for social causes. When it completed 50 years of existence it allocated a good amount of funds for celebration. Approximately ₹ 40 million was spent on society related initiatives. BEL has set up an Electronics Gallery at the Visvesvaraya Industrial and Technological Museum in Bangaluru and Chennai.

BEL encourages a culture of community initiative at its manufacturing unit level and ensures all employees take part in these initiatives.

Recent development

Bharat Electronics is forming some joint ventures to achieve technical excellence. Bharat Electronics Limited has set up a joint venture with General Electric (GE) USA, for manufacturing high voltage tanks and detector modules for computed tomography (CT) scan systems and advanced level of X-ray tubes. The company is in the process of joining with Bharat Heavy Electricals Limited (BHEL) to set up a joint venture to make solar photovoltaic components. BEL has signed a memorandum of understanding with Indus Teqsite, Chennai, for the design and development of digital subsystems for its equipment, test systems for its radars, avionics and electronic warfare, and another with the French company Thales International to set up a joint venture for civilian and defence radar. BEL has signed a memorandum of understanding with Textron Systems to provide micro-observer unattended ground sensor (UGS) systems to the Indian security agencies.

Customer Co-ordination Cell

Recently BEL has set up a Customer Co-ordination Cell. The customers of BEL comprise members of the Army, Navy, Air Force, paramilitary, Coast Guard (India, Seychelles, Maldives, Sri Lanka), Police, Doordarshan, All India Radio, Department of Telecommunications and consumers of professional electronic components are allowed to register their complaints with the Customer Co-ordination Cell by phone, fax or the Internet.

Container Corporation of India

Jump to navigation Jump to search

Container Corporation of India Limited

कॉनकॉर
CONCOR

Type	Public Sector Undertaking
Traded as	NSE: CONCOR BSE: 531344

Industry	Transport
Founded	March 1988
Headquarters	New Delhi, India
Key people	V. Kalyana Rama (Chairman & Managing Director)
Products	Terminals Intermodal
Revenue	▼ ₹ 6,473.79 crore (US$910 million) (2020)[1]
Operating income	▼ ₹ 523.96 crore (US$73 million) (2020)[1]
Net income	▼ ₹ 375.78 crore (US$53 million) (2020)
Total assets	▼ ₹ 11,566.78 crore (US$1.6 billion) (2020)
Total equity	▼ ₹ 10,064.74 crore (US$1.4 billion) (2020)[2]
Owner	Government of India (54.80%)
Number of employees	1,464 (March 2019)
Parent	Ministry of Railways (India)
Subsidiaries	CONCOR Air Ltd Fresh and Healthy Enterprise Limited Punjab Logistics Infrastructure Limited SIDCUL CONCOR Infra Company Ltd

Container Corporation of India Limited (CONCOR) is a Navratna Public Sector Undertaking under the Indian Ministry of Railways. Incorporated in March 1988 under the Companies Act, CONCOR commenced operations in November 1989 taking over an existing network of seven inland container depots (ICDs) from Indian Railways.

History

Indian Railway's strategic initiative to containerise cargo transport put India on the intermodal freight transport map for the first time in 1966. Given India's size (almost 3,000 kilometres (1,900 mi) from North to South and East to West), rail transport is often a cheaper option for all cargo over medium and long distances, especially if the cost of inter-modal transfers can be reduced. Seeing that containerised multi-modal door-to-door transport provided a solution to this problem, in 1966 Indian Railways entered the market for moving door-to-door domestic cargo in special DSO containers.

Although the first ISO container in India had been handled in Kochi as early as 1973, it was not until 1981 that the first ISO container was moved inland by Indian Railways to the country's first ICD at Bangaluru, also managed by the Indian Railways.

Expansion of the network to seven ICDs by 1988 saw an increase in container handling capacity, while along the way a strong view emerged that there was a need to set up a separate pro-active organisation to promote and manage the growth of containerisation in India.

Core Business

CONCOR operates three core businesses: cargo carrier; terminal operator, warehouse operator & MMLP operation.

Engineers India

Jump to navigation Jump to search

A Navratna Company

Type	Public Sector Undertaking
Traded as	BSE: 532178 NSE: ENGINERSIN
Industry	Engineering consulting EPC
Founded	1965
Headquarters	New Delhi, India
Key people	J C Nakra (Chairman & MD)

Revenue	▲₹3,203.05 crore (US$450 million) (2020)
Operating income	▲₹675.51 crore (US$95 million) (2020)
Net income	▲₹430.24 crore (US$60 million) (2020)
Total assets	▲₹5,028.80 crore (US$710 million) (2020)
Total equity	▲₹2,345.45 crore (US$330 million) (2020)
Owner	Government of India (51.50%)
Number of employees	2,806 (March 2020)
Website	engineersindia.com

Engineers India Limited (EIL) is a Navratna public-sector undertaking of the Government of India under the Ministry of Petroleum and Natural Gas. It was set up in 1965 to provide engineering and related technical services for petroleum refineries and other industrial projects.

EIL has its head office at Bhikaji Cama Place, New Delhi. EIL also has:

- an R&D complex at Gurgaon,
- a branch office at Mumbai,
- regional offices at Kolkata, Chennai, Vadodara,
- Inspection offices at all major equipment manufacturing locations in India.
- Overseas offices in London (England), Italy, Abu Dhabi and Malaysia.

EIL has two wholly owned subsidiaries, Ramagundam Fertilisers and Chemical Limited, Head Office in New Delhi and fertiliser and chemical plant in Ramagundam, Telangana, and Certification Engineers International Ltd, to undertake Independent Certification, and Third-Party Inspection (TPI) assignments.

Tata Projects Limited (TPL) and Engineers India Ltd (EIL) signed a Memorandum of Understanding (MoU) in July 2007 to incorporate a Joint-Venture (JV) Company which would undertake Engineering, Procurement and Construction (EPC) projects in India and abroad. The JV Company named TEIL Projects Limited was incorporated on 15 July 2008 in Delhi as a Public Limited Company (PLC).

EIL secured a Consultancy Services Contract from Bharat Petroleum Corporation Ltd (BPCL) for the Integrated Refinery Expansion Project (IREP) in Kochi at a fee of ₹ 720 crore on 6 July 2012.

Activities

- Petroleum refining
- Petrochemicals, chemicals and fertilisers
- Pipelines
- Offshore oil and gas
- Onshore oil and gas
- Terminals and storages
- Mining and metallurgy
- Infrastructure

It is diversifying into the following new areas:

- Water and waste management
- Infrastructure
- City gas distribution
- Power-thermal, solar & nuclear
- Gas-based fertiliser projects
- Coal to liquid (CTL)
- Steel
- Nuclear

The services offered by EIL include:

Pre-project services

- Feasibility studies
- Environment impact assessment
- Technology and process licensee selection
- Cost estimation

Project implementation services

- Project management
- Process design
- Detailed engineering
- Procurement

- Construction management
- Commissioning and plant start-up assistance

Specialist services

- Heat and Mass Transfer (HMT) equipment design
- Environment engineering
- Information Technology (IT)
- Specialist materials and maintenance
- Plant operations & safety including HAZOPS and risk analysis
- Refinery optimisation studies
- Yield and energy optimisation studies

Turnkey contracts

- Engineering
- Procurement
- Construction and commissioning

EIL has won a consultancy services contract from Cairn Energy India Pty Ltd for front end engineering and design for the Mangala Polymer Project involving creation of surface and infrastructure facilities for development of a polymer flood at Mangala for enhanced crude oil recovery

Completed projects

EIL has to its credit more than 5,000 assignments including over 400 major projects completed:

- 49 petroleum refinery projects
- 7 petrochemical complexes
- 37 pipeline projects
- 205 offshore platforms
- 35 oil and gas processing projects
- 26 mining and metallurgical projects
- 11 ports and terminals
- 8 fertiliser projects
- 26 infrastructure projects
- 17 LSTK projects

Hindustan Aeronautics Limited

> This article includes a list of general references, but it remains largely unverified because it lacks sufficient corresponding inline citations. Please help to improve this article by introducing more precise citations. (May 2017) (Learn how and when to remove this template message)

Hindustan Aeronautics Limited

Type	Public Sector Undertaking
Traded as	NSE: HAL BSE: / 541154
Industry	Aerospace and Defence
Founded	1940; 80 years ago (As Hindustan Aircraft) 1964; 56 years ago (Renamed Hindustan Aeronautics)
Headquarters	Bangaluru, Karnataka, India
Key people	R Madhavan (Chairman & MD)
Products	Transport aircraft Fighter aircraft Helicopters
Revenue	▲₹21,522.07 crore (US$3.0 billion) (2020)
Operating income	▲₹3,960.57 crore (US$560 million) (2020)
Net income	▲₹2,857.02 crore (US$400 million) (2020)
Total assets	▲₹53,120.49 crore (US$7.4 billion) (2020)
Total equity	▲₹13,215.12 crore (US$1.9 billion) (2020)
Owner	Government of India (89.97%)
Number of employees	28,345 (April 2019)
Website	hal-india.co.in

Hindustan Aeronautics Limited (HAL) is an Indian state-owned aerospace and defence company headquartered in Bangaluru (Bengaluru), India. It is governed under the management of the Indian Ministry of Defence.

The government-owned corporation is primarily involved in the operations of the aerospace and is currently involved in the design, fabrication and assembly of aircraft, jet engines, helicopters and their spare parts. It has several facilities spread across India including Bangalore, Nasik, Korwa, Kanpur, Koraput, Lucknow, Hyderabad, Barrackpore and Kasaragod. The HAL HF-24 Marut fighter-bomber was the first fighter aircraft made in India.

History

HAL was established as Hindustan Aircraft Limited in Bangaluru on 23 December 1940 by Walchand Hirachand who became Chairman of the company. The company's office was opened at a banglow called "Eventice" on Domlur Road.

The organisation and equipment for the factory at Bangaluru was set up by William D. Pawley of the Intercontinental Aircraft Corporation of New York. Pawley obtained a large number of machine-tools and equipment from the United States.

The Indian Government bought a one-third stake in the company and by April 1941 by investing ₹ 25 lakh as it believed this to be a strategic imperative. The decision by the government was primarily motivated to boost British military hardware supplies in Asia to counter the increasing threat posed by Imperial Japan during Second World War. The Kingdom of Mysore supplied two directors, Air Marshal John Higgins was resident director. The first aircraft built was a Harlow PC-5. On 2 April 1942, the government announced that the company had been nationalised when it had bought out the stakes of Seth Walchand Hirachand and other promoters so that it could act freely. The Mysore Kingdom refused to sell its stake in the company but yielded the management control over to the Indian Government.

The total number of broad-gauge coaches manufactured by the Hindustan Aircraft Limited during the year 1954 is 158.

In 1943, the Bangaluru factory was handed over to the United States Army Air Forces but still using Hindustan Aircraft management.

The factory expanded rapidly and became the centre for major overhaul and repair of American aircraft and was known as the 84th Air Depot. The first aircraft to be overhauled was a Consolidated PBY Catalina followed by every type of aircraft operated in India and Burma. When returned to Indian control two years later the factory had become one of the largest overhaul and repair organisations in the East. In the post war reorganisation the company built railway carriages as an interim activity.

After India gained independence in 1947, the management of the company was passed over to the Government of India.

Hindustan Aeronautics Limited (HAL) was formed on 1 October 1964 when Hindustan Aircraft Limited joined the consortium formed in June by the IAF Aircraft Manufacturing Depot, Kanpur (at the time manufacturing HS-748 under licence) and the group recently set up to manufacture MiG-21 under licence, with its new factories planned in Koraput, Nasik and Hyderabad. Though HAL was not used actively for developing newer models of fighter jets, except for the HF-24 Marut, the company has played a crucial role in modernisation of the Indian Air Force. In 1957 company started manufacturing Bristol Siddeley Orpheus jet engines under licence at new factory located in Bangalore.

During the 1980s, HAL's operations saw a rapid increase which resulted in the development of new indigenous aircraft such as the HAL Tejas and HAL Dhruv. HAL also developed an advanced version of the Mikoyan-Gurevich MiG-21, known as MiG-21 Bison, which increased its life-span by more than 20 years. HAL has also obtained several multimillion-dollar contracts from leading international aerospace firms such as Airbus, Boeing and Honeywell to manufacture aircraft spare parts and engines.

By 2012, HAL was reportedly bogged down in the details of production and has been slipping on its schedules. On 1 April 2015, HAL reconstituted its Board with TS Raju as CMD, S Subrahmanyan as Director (Operations), VM Chamola as Director (HR), CA Ramana Rao as Director (Finance) and D K Venkatesh as Director (Engineering & R&D). There are two government nominees in the board and six independent directors.

In March 2017, HAL Chairman and Managing Director T Suvarna Raju announced that the company had finalised plans for an indigenisation drive. The company plans to produce nearly 1,000 military helicopters, including Kamov 226, LCH (Light Combat Helicopter), ALH (Advanced Light Helicopter), and over 100 planes over the next 10 years. HAL will manufacture the Kamov 226T helicopter under a joint venture agreement with Russian defence manufacturers. The Kamov 226T will replace the country's fleet of Cheetah and Chetak helicopters. Over the next 5 years, HAL will carry out major upgrade of almost the entire fighter fleet of Indian Air Force including Su-30MKI, Jaguars, Mirage and Hawk jets to make them "more lethal". The company will also deliver 123 Tejas Light Combat Aircraft to the IAF from 2018–19, at a rate of 16 jets per year. LCH production will now take place in a newly built Light Combat Helicopter Production Hangar at Helicopter Division in HAL Complex.

In view of Make in India policy and to increase the share of defence exports to achieve the target of $5 billion dollars by 2025, HAL is planning to setup logistic bases in Indonesia, Malaysia, Sri Lanka and Vietnam with priority target for Southeast Asia, West Asia and North African markets. It would not only help to promote HAL products but also act as service centre for Soviet/Russian origin equipment.

Operations

One of the largest aerospace companies in Asia, HAL has annual turnover of over US$2 billion. More than 40% of HAL's revenues come from international deals to manufacture aircraft engines, spare parts, and other aircraft materials. A partial list of major operations undertaken by HAL includes the following:

International agreements

Bangalore

- The US$35 billion fifth-generation fighter jet programme with the Sukhoi Corporation of Russia.
- US$1 billion contract to manufacture aircraft parts for Boeing.
- Multi-role transport aircraft project with Ilyushin of Russia worth US$600 million.
- 120 RD-33MK turbofan engines to be manufactured for MiG-29K by HAL for US$250 million.

- Contract to manufacture 1,000 TPE331 aircraft engines for Honeywell worth US$200,000 each (estimates put total value of deal at US$200 million).
- US$120 million deal to manufacture Dornier 228 for RUAG of Switzerland.
- Manufacture of aircraft parts for Airbus SAS worth US$150 million.
- US$100 million contract to export composite materials to Israel Aircraft Industries.
- US$65 million joint-research facility with Honeywell and planned production of Garrett TPE331 engines.
- US$50.7 million contract to supply Advanced Light Helicopter to Ecuadorian Air Force. HAL will also open a maintenance base in the country.
- US$30 million contract to supply avionics for Malaysian Su-30MKM.
- US$20 million contract to supply ambulance version of HAL Dhruv to Peru.
- Contract of 3 HAL Dhruv helicopters from Turkey worth US$20 million.
- US$10 million order from Namibia for HAL Chetak and Cheetah helicopters.
- Supply of HAL Dhruv helicopters to Mauritius' National Police in a deal worth US$7 million.
- Unmanned helicopter development project with Israel Aircraft Industries.

Domestic agreements

- 220 Sukhoi Su-30MKI being manufactured at HAL's facilities in Nasik, Koraput and Bangalore. The total contract, which also involves Russia's Sukhoi Aerospace, is worth US$3.2 billion.
- 200 HAL Light Combat Helicopters for the Indian Air Force and 500 HAL Dhruv helicopters worth US$5.83 billion.
- US$900 million aerospace hub in Shamshabad, Telangana.
- US$57 million upgrade of SEPECAT Jaguar fleet of the Indian Air Force.

- US$55 million helicopter simulator training facility in Bangaluru in collaboration with Canada's CAE.
- 64 MiG-29s to be upgraded by HAL and Russia's MiG Corporation in a programme worth US$960 million.
- Licenced production of 82 BAe Hawk 132.

Indigenous products

Over the years, HAL has designed and developed several platforms like the HAL HF-24 Marut, HAL Advance Light Helicopter Dhruv, HAL Light Utility Helicopter, HAL Light Combat Helicopter to name a few. HAL also manufactures indigenous products with technology transferred from the DRDO, in association with Bharat Electronics for its avionics and Indian Ordnance Factories for the on-board weapons systems and ammunition.

HAL supplies ISRO, the integrated L-40 stages for GSLV Mk II, propellant tanks, feed lines of PSLV, GSLV MKII and GSLV MKIII launch vehicles and structures of various satellites.

Agricultural aircraft

- HF-24 Marut — (retired) Mk.1 and Mk.1T (200+ built)
- Tejas — (in production) Mk.1, Mk.1A, NLCA Mk.1 and NLCA Mk.2 (40+ built)
- Tejas Mk.2 (MWF) — Medium weight fighter (under development) 2023 first flight expected.
- AMCA — Fifth generation stealth fighter (under development).
- TEDBF — Twin Engine Deck Based Fighter is 4.5 generation fighter for Indian Navy's aircraft carrier. (under development) [40]

Helicopters

- Dhruv — (in production) Advanced Light Helicopter (350+ built)
- Rudra — (in production) Attack helicopter (70+ built)
- Light Combat Helicopter — (in production)Attack helicopter (10+ built)

- Light Utility Helicopter (under trial)
- Indian Multi-role Helicopter (under development)

Engines

- GTX-35VS Kaveri — co-developed with GTRE (DRDO) (under development; developed into following programmes)
- PTAE-7 — For indigenously designed Lakshya PTA
- GTSU-110 — for starting main engine GE404 or Kaveri of LCA Tejas
- Shakti — co-developed with Turbomeca for HAL Dhruv Helicopter to be used in light utility helicopter
- HTFE-25
- HTSE-1200 (under development)

Trainer aircraft

HJT-16 Kiran

- HT-2 — First Company design to enter production.
- HPT-32 Deepak — Basic trainer in service for more than three decades.
- HJT-16 Kiran — Mk1, Mk1A and Mk2 - Turbojet trainers scheduled to be replaced with HJT-36 Sitara.
- HTT-34 — Turboprop version of HPT-32 Deepak.
- HTT-35 — Proposed replacement for HPT-32 basic trainer in the early 1990s; not pursued.
- HJT-36 Sitara — Intermediate jet trainer (under development).
- HTT-40 Basic trainer (in production)[first prototype flew its first flight on 31 May 2016.(106 ordered)
- HJT 39 / CAT Advanced jet trainer (proposal).

Observation and reconnaissance aircraft

- HAOP-27 Krishak

Transport and passenger aircraft

- Saras — (in production) multi-purpose civilian light transport aircraft.

- Multirole Transport Aircraft (now called Ilyushin Il-276) — under joint-development with Ilyushin Design Bureau. HAL is no longer an active partner.
- Indian Regional Jet (IRJ) of 70-100 seater capacity to be jointly developed with NAL.

Utility aircraft

Gliders

- HAL G-1 — HAL's first original design, dating from 1941. Only one was built.
- Ardhra — training glider
- Rohini

Unmanned Aerial Vehicles

PTA Lakshya — UAV

- PTA Lakshya 2 — UAV
- NRUAV
- Nishant UAV
- Rustom H – Unmanned Aerial Vehicle
- UCAV Tejas — Unmanned Combat Aerial Vehicle (under development)

Licenced production

- Vampire — first combat jet manufactured by HAL, 250+ FB.52, 60 T.55 models
- Harlow PC-5 — first aircraft assembled by HAL
- Percival Prentice — 66 built by HAL
- Mikoyan-Gurevich MiG-21 — FL, M, Bis and Bison upgrades variants 660 built by HAL
- Folland Gnat
- Ajeet — improved version of the Folland Gnat
- Mikoyan-Gurevich MiG-27 — M variant
- SEPECAT Jaguar— IS, IB and IM variants
- BAE Hawk — scheduled production run of 42 aircraft
- Sukhoi Su-30MKI — a derivative of the Sukhoi Su-30

- Dornier Do 228 — 117 built + fuselage, wings and tail unit for production of the upgraded Do 228 NG variant
- Aerospatiale SA 315B Lama — HAL Cheetah, Lancer, Cheetal Variants
- Aerospatiale SA 316B Alouette III — HAL Chetak, Chetan Variants
- HS 748 Avro — Modified for military usage, includes Series 2M variant with large freight door
- Rolls-Royce Turbomeca Adour Mk 811 — Engine for SEPECAT Jaguar
- Rolls-Royce Turbomeca Adour Mk 871 — Engine for BAE Hawk Mk 132
- Garrett TPE331-5 — Engine for Dornier Do 228
- Turbomeca TM 333 — Engine for HAL Dhruv

Notable people

- Kota Harinarayana
- Kurt Tank
- Roddam Narasimha
- Vishnu Madav Ghatage

See also

- Companies portal
  - HAL Aerospace Museum
  - Defence Research and Development Organisation
  - HAL Airport
  - Indian Space Research Organisation
  - Central Aircraft Manufacturing Company
  - Hindustan Aeronautics Limited SC
  - National Aerospace Laboratories
  - Mahindra Aerospace
  - Tata Advanced Systems
  - Aeronautical Development Agency

Mahanagar Telephone Nigam Limited

Formerly	Bombay Telephone Limited
Type	Subsidiary of Bharat Sanchar Nigam Limited
Traded as	BSE: 500108 NSE: MTNL
ISIN	INE153A01019
Industry	Telecommunications
Founded	1 April 1986; 34 years ago
Founder	Government of India
Headquarters	Mahanagar Doorsanchar Sadan, 9, CGO Complex, Lodhi Road, New Delhi, India
Areas served	Delhi NCR, Navi Mumbai, Thane (India) Mauritius Nepal
Key people	Sunil Kumar (Chairman & MD)
Products	Mobile telephony Fixed-line telephony Digital television Wired and Wireless Broadband IPTV
Revenue	▼ ₹3,116.42 crore (US$440 million) (FY18)
Operating income	▼ ₹-2,973.45 crore (US$−420 million) (FY18)
Net income	▼ ₹-2,973.03 crore (US$−420 million) (FY18)
Total assets	▼ ₹16,249.66 crore (US$2.3 billion) (FY18)
Total equity	▼ ₹-6,337.35 crore (US$−890 million) (FY18)
Number of employees	25,191 (FY18)
Parent	Bharat Sanchar Nigam Limited[
Subsidiaries	Mahanagar Telephone Mauritius Limited (MTML) United Telecoms Limited
Website	www.mtnl.in mtnldelhi.in mtnlmumbai.in

Mahanagar Telephone Nigam Limited, d/b/a MTNL, is a state-owned telecommunications service provider and wholly owned subsidiary of BSNL headquartered in New Delhi, India. MTNL provides services in the metro cities of Mumbai and New Delhi in India and in the island nation of Mauritius in Africa. The company had a monopoly in Mumbai and New Delhi until 1992, when the telecom sector was opened to other service providers. "Transparency makes us different" is the motto of the company. The Government of India currently holds 57% stock in the company with the rest being held by public and institutional investors. The company's shares are listed on Bombay Stock Exchange, Global depository receipts on London Stock Exchange and American depository receipts on New York Stock Exchange. As of March 2020, it has 3.35 million subscribers. It is also a public sector enterprise of Navratna status which is given by Government of India to the best performing state owned companies.

The company's name derives from Hindi: *Mahanagar* meaning "metropolis" (*maha* "big", *nagar* "city") and *nigam* meaning "corporation".

History

Bombay Telephone was founded in 1882. The first telephone exchange in Mumbai began operations on 28 January 1882. Delhi's first telephone system was established in 1911. Mahanagar Telephone Nigam was created by the Government of India in 1986 to oversee the telephone services of Delhi and Mumbai.

Products

MTNL provides fixed line telephones and WLL services. It also provides mobile services on GSM and CDMA platforms. MTNL various service brands are:

Dolphin – a postpaid GSM service which also provides value added services such as 3G,

Trump – a prepaid GSM service, similar to Dolphin,

Garuda – a WLL service which provides an *FW* tariff, and a *Mobile* tariff.

Phone numbers belonging to MTNL start with the prefix 2 in fixed line telephones and WLL. In GSM, mobile numbers start with the prefixes 901x, 9868, 9757, 9869, 9968, and 9969.

MTNL's efficiency has drastically improved over the years. In the past, a customer had to wait much longer to secure a connection but now he/she can receive a connection within hours of the subscription request being filed.

Radio frequency summary

MTNL owns spectrum in 850 MHz, 900 MHz, 1800 MHz, and 2100 MHz bands across the country.

Telecom circle coverage	*FD-LTE 850MHz Band 5*	*E-GSM 900MHz Band 8*	*GSM / FD-LTE 1800MHz Band 3*	*UMTS 2100MHz Band 1*
Delhi	✓	✓	✓	✓
Mumbai	✓	✓	✓	✓

3G Mobile Service

MTNL started 3G services in India under the name of "MTNL 3G Jadoo." Services offered include video calling, mobile TV and mobile broadband with high speed data connectivity up to 3.6 Mbit/s from 11 December 2008. MTNL plans to offer 3G services across India by mid-2009. MTNL also provides 3G data cards for usage in devices other than mobile phones. MTNL will be installing 15 lakh 3G lines in the first phase of its 3G roll-out in Mumbai and Delhi (which currently have 40 lakh existing mobile lines). MTNL announced in Jan, 2012 that they will upgrade its 3G network to more advanced HSPA+ with download speeds up to 28.8 Mbit/s before the end of 2012.

MTNL rolled out its BlackBerry solutions on the 2G and 3G networks by launching India's first 3G-enabled BlackBerry Bold smart phones.

Broadband and FTTH

MTNL is the largest ISP in Mumbai and Delhi (in terms of market share), and the third largest ISP in India though it has presence just in two circles. MTNL provides *TriBand* Internet services through dialup and DSL. It provides games on demand, video on demand, and IPTV services in India through *TriBand.* TriBand is targeted at homes and small businesses.

MTNL began offering fibre-to-the-home (FTTH) triple play (voice, video, and data) high speed broadband service in Delhi on 9 November

2011. FTTH, with core network speed up to 1 Gbit/s, was launched in Mumbai on 1 March 2012. MTNL FTTH Broadband offers several services based on triple play services like IPTV, HDTV, and 3DTV, video on demand, bandwidth on demand, instant video conferencing, interactive gaming and several other value added services.

In 2004, telecom regulator TRAI mandated a minimum speed of 256 Kbit/s for all broadband connections. MTNL increased the minimum speed of all its broadband plans to 512 Kbit/s from existing 256 Kbit/s, effective 26 January 2012, becoming the first ISP in India to opt for a minimum broadband speed from 256 Kbit/s to 512 Kbit/s, without any mandatory regulation. On 12 November 2013, MTNL announced that it would upgrade the speed of all its existing unlimited broadband plans in Mumbai to a minimum of 1 Mbit/s, at no additional cost.

MTNL also provides other services such as VPN, VOIP, and leased lines through BSNL and VSNL.

Mahanagar Telephone Mauritius Limited (MTML)

MTNL has set up a wholly owned subsidiary called Mahanagar Telephone Mauritius Limited (MTML) in Mauritius, providing mobile and international long distance services. MTML is the second operator in Mauritius. Necessary licences were obtained in January 2004. MTML has already started its ILD & CDMA based basic services in Mauritius. In Mauritius, 44,312 telephone connections are operational from a total switching capacity of 50,000. Moreover, through joint ventures with local telecommunications providers, MTML plans to offer Internet access through its wireless network by February 2007.

Merger with BSNL

On the 23rd day of October 2019, the Government of India announced revival package for BSNL and MTNL which includes monetising assets, raising funds, TD-LTE spectrum, voluntary retirement scheme for employees. Apart from package, Ministry of Communications decided to merge of MTNL with Bharat Sanchar Nigam Limited. Pending this, MTNL will be subsidiary of BSNL.

Joint Ventures

MTNL-STPI IT Services Ltd. is a 50:50 joint venture between Software Technology Parks of India (STPI) and Mahanagar Telephone Nigam Limited, (MTNL).

Millennium Telecom Limited (MTL)

MTNL has restructured Millennium Telecom Ltd. (MTL) as a joint venture company of MTNL and BSNL with 50% and 50% equity participation respectively. The company will now be entering into new business stream of international long distance operations and will be executing a project of submarine cable system, both east and west from India.

Telephone Advisory Committees

Telephone Advisory Committees also known as TAC is an Indian Government body made up of Members of Parliament and nominated members by the Ministry of Communications and Information Technology (India) to address issues concerning telecommunication in India. Looked upon as a privileged panel, the Telephone Advisory Committees (TAC), constituted by the Ministry of Communications and Information Technology (India) of the Government of India to serve as a vital feedback mechanism for improvement of services in the Telecommunications sector by the Department of Telecommunications.

List of TAC Members

A

- Anandrao Vithoba Adsul
- Hansraj Gangaram Ahir
- Ramdas Athawale

B

- E. T. Mohammed Basheer
- Shadi Lal Batra
- Bodh Singh Bhagat

- Subhash Bhamre
- Balwinder Singh Bhunder
- Ranjit Singh Brahmpura

C

- Prem Singh Chandumajra
- Santokh Singh Chaudhary
- Dushyant Chautala
- Jitendra Choudhury

D

- Husain Dalwai
- Sankar Prasad Datta
- Anil Desai
- Dharambir
- Rajkumar Dhoot
- Sanjay Shamrao Dhotre
- Jyoti Dhurve

G

- Dharamvir Gandhi
- Ashok Sekhar Ganguly
- Heena Gavit
- Sher Singh Ghubaya
- M. S. Gill
- Naresh Gujral

H

- Deepender Singh Hooda

J

- Prataprao Ganpatrao Jadhav

K

- P. Karunakaran
- Rattan Lal Kataria

- Chandrakant Khaire
- Avinash Rai Khanna
- Vinod Khanna
- Kirron Kher
- Gajanan Kirtikar
- Ashwani Kumar
- Selja Kumari
- Keny Sanjay Govind

L

- Sadashiv Lokhande

M

- Bhagwant Mann
- Majeed Memon

N

- Shantaram Naik
- C.P. Narayanan

P

- Chikki Panday
- Praful Patel
- Rajni Patil
- Nanabhau Patole
- Sharad Pawar

R

- Poonam Mahajan
- Sanjay Raut
- Rekha
- Charanjeet Singh Rori
- C. L. Ruala

S

- A. Sampath

- Vijay Sampla
- Alok Sanjar
- T. N. Seema
- Arvind Kumar Sharma
- Gopal Shetty
- Rahul Shewale
- Rajeev Shukla
- Sukhdev Singh Dhindsa
- Amarinder Singh
- Sadhu Singh
- Virendra Singh (Mirzapur)
- Raj Kumar Saini
- Wansuk Syiem

T

- Shashi Tharoor
- Ronald Sapa Tlau
- D. P. Tripathi

National Aluminum Company

From Wikipedia, the free encyclopedia

Jump to navigationJump to search

National Aluminum Company Limited

नालको NALCO

Type	Public Sector Undertaking
Traded as	NSE: NATIONALUM BSE: 532234
Industry	Mining Power
Headquarters	Bhubaneswar, Odisha, India
Key people	Sridhar Patra (Chairman & MD)

Products	Bauxite Aluminum Alumina Hydrate
Revenue	▼₹8,471.84 crore (US$1.2 billion) (2020)
Operating income	▼₹226.24 crore (US$32 million) (2020)
Net income	▼₹138.23 crore (US$19 million) (2020)
Total assets	▼₹14,549.62 crore (US$2.0 billion) (2020)
Total equity	▼₹9,988.07 crore (US$1.4 billion) (2020)
Owner	Government of India (51.50%)[*]
Number of employees	6,496 (April 2019)
Website	nalcoindia.com

National Aluminum Company Limited, abbreviated as **NALCO,** (incorporated in 1981) is a Navratna group 'A' CPSE having integrated and diversified operations in mining, metal and power under Ministry of Mines, Government of India. Presently, Government of India holds a 51.5% equity in NALCO.

It is one of the largest integrated Bauxite-Alumina-Aluminum-Power Complex in the country encompassing bauxite mining, alumina refining, aluminum smelting and casting, power generation, rail and port operations.

The Company is the lowest-cost producer of metallurgical grade alumina in the World and lowest-cost producer of Bauxite in the world as per Wood McKenzie report. With sustained quality products, the Company's export earnings accounted for about 42% of the sales turnover in the year 2018-19 and the Company is rated as 3rd highest net export earning CPSE as per Public Enterprise Survey report.

To face the challenges of ever-evolving market and position the Company in a sustainable growth path, a new corporate plan has been developed with well-defined 3 year action plan, 7 year strategy and 15 years vision of being a Premier and Integrated Company in the Aluminum value chain with strategic presence in Mining both domestic and global, Metals and Energy sectors. The Corporate Plan has chalked out a roadmap for multifold growth in revenue and Profit by 2032.

As a responsive Corporate, the Company is harnessing renewable energy aligning to the ambitious programmes of Govt. of India. The

Company has already commissioned 198 MW wind power plants and further 50 MW wind power plants are in pipeline, making it the highest producer of renewable energy among PSUs.

Operations

NALCO is headquartered at Bhubaneswar, Odisha.

NALCO operates from two major Units

- Mining and Refinery (M&R) complex
  - Bauxite Mines located at Panchpatmali hills, Koraput with capacity of 6825,000 TPA
  - Alumina Refinery located at Damanjodi, Odisha with capacity of 2275,000 TPA
- Smelter and Power (S&P) complex
  - Aluminium Smelter located at Angul, Odisha with capacity of 460,000 TPA
  - Captive Power Plant located at Angul, Odisha with capacity of 1200 MW
- Port Facilities at Visakhapatnam and Paradip.
- Wind Power Plants
  - Gandikota, Andhra Pradesh - 50.4 MW (2.1 MW, 24 nos. WEGs)
  - Ludarwa, Jaisalmer, Rajasthan - 47.6 MW (0.85 MW, 56 nos. WEGs)
  - Devikot, Jaisalmer, Rajasthan - 50 MW (2 MW, 25 nos. WEG)
  - Sangli, Maharashtra - 50.4 MW (2.1 MW, 24 nos. WEGs)
- Solar Power at Nalco Corporate Office, Bhubaneswar & NALCO Research & Technology Center, Bhubaneswar
- Regional offices at Kolkata, Mumbai, Delhi, Chennai and Bangalore
- 10 operating stockyards at various locations in the Country

Products

Main products of NALCO are as follows:

Aluminium Metal

- Ingots
- Alloy Ingots

- T-Ingots
- Sows
- Billets
- Wire Rods
- Cast strips

Alumina and Hydrate

- Calcined Alumina
- Alumina Hydrate

Rolled Product

- Aluminium Rolled Products
- Aluminium Chequered Sheets

Power

- Thermal Power
- Co-generation Power
- Wind Power
- Solar Power

Employees

As on June 2019, there were 6,385 employees on the Company's roll.

Expansions

- To be more resilient to the vagaries of market, the Company has prepared a New All-Weather Business Model. It has extensive plans for brownfield and Greenfield expansion projects, which include the ongoing 5th Stream Refinery project of 1 MTPA capacity in existing Alumina Refinery at Damanjodi (Brownfield), development of Pottangi bauxite mines, Utkal D&E coal mines in Odisha, establishment 5 lakh TPA brownfield Smelters in Odisha.
- As part of backward integration, the Company is establishing a caustic soda plant in JV with Gujarat Alkalies & Chemicals Limited (GACL) in Gujarat and a CT Pitch plant in JV with NINL in Odisha.
- The Company has formed JV Company named 'Angul Aluminium Park Private Ltd' (AAPPL) with Odisha Industrial

Infrastructure Development Corporation (IDCO) to give a boost to ancillary, upstream and downstream products related to aluminum industry.

Research and Development

- NALCO Research and Technology Centre (NRTC) is located at Bhubaneswar, Odisha.
- The Company pursues its R&D activities fervently and has already filed 36 patents out of which 17 patents have been granted and 5 have been commercialised till Dec 2018. As a part of its effort to convert waste to wealth, the Company is endeavouring to salvage iron concentrate from red mud, Gallium from spent liquor. The Company has also successfully commissioned a first of its kind de-fluoridation process based on nano-technology to de-contaminate the effluent water of smelter solving a long standing fluoride contamination problem of the area.

Mobile Apps

NALCO has developed four mobile apps:

1. Nisarg - Nalco Initiatives for Social Awareness and Responsible Growth
2. Naginaa - Nalco Grahak Information and Networking App for All
3. Namasya - Nalco Micro and Small enterprise Yogayog Application
4. Hamesha Nalconian - App for the Retired employees of NALCO

CSR

- The Company, while climbing the ladder of success has strived hard to play a significant role in the socio-economic development in its operational areas through empathetic CSR activities. Rehabilitation of displaced families, employment, income generation, healthcare and sanitation of local people, education and skill development, providing safe drinking water, development of infrastructure, pollution control, environmental measures, rural development, promotion of arts, crafts and culture and various humanitarian good will missions have earned NALCO a place of pride in the corporate world and was awarded the SCOPE Meritorious Award for CSR from Hon'ble President of India in April 1917.

- For effective implementation of CSR activities, NALCO has set up a standalone Foundation in 2010.
- It has spent ₹ 325 crore towards CSR activities till 2017-2018.
- Notable efforts in field of Education includes Indradhanush scheme, where the Company has sponsored 920 tribal children of Maoist infested Damanjodi sector and provided education to them in 3 reputed residential schools. 416 meritorious girl students of BPL families at Angul and Damanjodi sector have been adopted with financial support by the Company under 'Nalco ki Ladli' scheme in line with Govt's 'Beti Bachao, Beti Padhao' Mission.
- Recognising the healthcare needs as one of the critical need, NALCO is operating 8 MHUs (Mobile Health Units) in peripheral villages of its plants by which more than one lakh patients are treated freely every year. Going a step ahead, the Company is also setting a secondary modern eye care hospital at Angul and a Night Shelter in AIIMS, Bhubaneswar for attendants of indoor and OPD patients availing long term treatment.
- Responding to the call of Govt. of India, NALCO actively participated in Swachh Bharat Abhiyan by constructing 479 toilets in various districts of its operating areas and has also taken up a noble initiative to make 11 periphery villages completely Open Defecation Free (ODF) in Damanjodi and Angul sector.
- The Company has taken the responsibility of Shri Jagannath Temple, Puri and its surrounding under PM's Iconic Shrine Development Programme to upgrade the infrastructure and maintain cleanliness with special emphasis on Renovation and beautification of Gandhi Park as a tourist spot, temple illumination, beautification of Puri town with thematic painting based on Jagannatha culture and battery-operated vehicle in railway station for differently-abled passengers and sick people.

- First Mines Safety Award-1988 by DGMS
- Best Eco-friendly Factory Award 1994–95 to the Mines and Refinery Complex by Odisha State Factory Inspectorate
- State Award-1995 to Captive Power Plant from state Factory inspectorate for Environment Management
- Indira Priyadarshini Vrikshamitra Award-1994 from MOEF, Govt. of India, for afforestation and wasteland development
- FICCI Environment Award for Environment Conservation and Pollution Control- 1996–97
- WEC-IIEE-IAEWP Environment award -1997 for contributing towards environment protection
- Gem Granite Environment Award for -1997-98 by FIMI, New Delhi for Mines
- Shri Sita Ram Rungta Memorial Social Awareness Award-1997-98 by FIMI, New Delhi
- Pollution Control Excellence Award – 1998 by Odisha State Pollution Control Board for Mines
- Special Commendation under Golden Peacock Environment Management Award 1998 Scheme by World Environment Foundation
- State Award for Best Occupational Health Centre to S&P Complex-1998
- Best Safety Performance Award to CPP by CII (ER)- 1999–2000
- The prestigious Dun & Bradstreet's Best PSU Award – 2012 in Non-Ferrous Metal Category.[5]
- Outstanding CSR Practices in Community Development – Odisha CSR Summit 2016.

Right to Information Act

Since NALCO is a public authority, it comes under the Right to Information Act. Thus, NALCO is required to provide information to various RTI queries asked by general public.

See also

- List of countries by aluminium production
- List of alumina refineries
- List of aluminium smelters

References

Jump up to:[a b c d e] "Balance Sheet 31.03.2020".

1. ^ "Latest Shareholding Pattern - National Aluminium Company Ltd". trendlyne.com. Retrieved 7 August 2020.
2. ^ https://nalcoindia.com/wp-content/uploads/2019/08/Annual-Report_38th-AGM.pdf
3. "Latest Shareholding Pattern - National Aluminium Company Ltd". Trendlyne.com. Retrieved 7 August 2020.
4. "Nalco gets D&B best PSU award". 2 June 2012.
5. "No information on corruption in Nalco: RTI reply". 5 November 2013. Retrieved 5 November 2013.
6. "Information Philosophy in NALCO". Retrieved 5 November 2013.

External links

- Official website

NBCC (India) Limited

Type	Public Sector Undertaking
Traded as	BSE: 534309 NSE: NBCC
Founded	1960 (Delhi, India)
Headquarters	Delhi, India
Key people	P K Gupta (Chairman & MD)
Revenue	▼₹5,210.34 crore (US$730 million) (2020)
Operating income	▼₹247.94 crore (US$35 million) (2020)
Net income	▼₹79.87 crore (US$11 million) (2020)
Total assets	▼₹7,765.38 crore (US$1.1 billion) (2020)
Total equity	▼₹1,523.60 crore (US$210 million) (2020)

Owner	Government of India (61.75%)
Number of employees	1,847 (March 2019) [3]
Subsidiaries	Hospital Services Consultancy Corporation India Limited Hindustan Steelworks Construction Limited (HSCL)
Website	www.nbccindia.com

NBCC (India) Limited (formerly National Buildings Construction Corporation Limited) is a blue-chip Government of India Navratna enterprise and a Central Public Sector Undertaking which trades publicly in the market. The Company's present areas of operations are categorised into three main segments, i.e. (i) Project Management Consultancy (PMC), including redevelopment of government properties, (ii) Engineering, Procurement & Construction (EPC) and (iii) Real Estate Development.

NBCC acquired 100 per cent stake in Mini Ratna hospital consultancy firm Hospital Services Consultancy Corporation Limited (HSCC) from Ministry of Health and Family Welfare on 6 November 2018. The organisation acquired over 51% stake in Hindustan Steelworks Construction Limited (HSCL), a PSU under the Steel Ministry in 2017.

NBCC is headquartered in New Delhi and it has 31 regional offices across India. The projects undertaken by the company are located across India and in countries such as Iraq, Libya, Nepal, Mauritius, Turkey, Botswana, Maldives, Yemen, Oman, UAE, Dubai and Africa. The organisation has executed several landmark projects that include re-development of government properties, construction of Roads, Railway Stations, Hospitals & Medical Colleges, Institutions, Offices, Bridges, and Industrial & Environmental Structures.

NBCC is designated as the implementing agency for executing projects under the Atal Mission for Rejuvenation and Urban Transformation (AMRUT), Pradhan Mantri Gram Sadak Yojna (PMGSY), Solid Waste Management (SWM) and developmental work in North Eastern Region.

NBCC is also working as Project Management Consultant (PMC) for the redevelopment of Pragati Maidan project of India Trade

Promotion Organisation. A number of Central Government ministries and various State Governments have been utilising the services of NBCC as their extended engineering arm.

Functional setup

NBCC has its Corporate Office at New Delhi which works as a policy-maker, planner and overall controller. Corporate functions are managed through various organisational divisions viz. Project Management Group, Business Development, Real Estate, Vigilance, Contract Engineering, Law, Centralised Procurement Group (CPG), Finance, Corporate communication, Personnel & Administration.

The work of the corporation is further decentralised into various Regional Business Groups (RBGs), Strategic Business Groups (SBGs), Zones, Units and Sites. RBG/SBG/Zones are controlled by executives of the rank of ED/CGM/GM respectively who directly reports to the Director(s) sitting in HO.

Regional Business Groups and Strategic Business Group headquarters are located at Delhi as well as at other places in all the states depending upon the quantum and the nature of the projects. RBGs are headed by Executive Director; SBGs by CGM & Zones are headed by GM/AGM and are assisted in their work by Technical, Finance & P&A Staff of appropriate level. RBGs/SBGs/Zones control and look after several projects which are headed by Unit-in-Charges.

Each project is a profit centre and is expected to operate efficiently to achieve turnover targets and profitability as per MoU signed between the corporate office and the RBG/SBG/Zonal Heads. The units are headed by an officer of the rank of AGM/DGM/PM/DPM/SPE. The Unit In-charge is responsible for efficient execution of a project and within approved cost who is assisted by other Technical staff depending upon the nature and value of project. The unit In-charge, from time to time, appraises the Zonal In-charge about providing the requisite inputs / resources required for the execution of the work.

Project site is controlled by a Site In-charge. The project is provided with the required number of technical staff. The site in-charge is responsible for efficient execution of the project ensuring its timely completion.

The Job Description and Duties and Responsibilities of various Heads are given below:

(A) RBG/SBG/Zonal Heads

1. Achieve turnover target within the specified cost/time for delivery of determined profit.
2. Function strictly as per the delegation of powers/financial rules in the matter of award of work and purchase of articles/goods, machines/equipments relating to works and establishment.
3. Maintain discipline and administrative efficiency in all the offices within the jurisdiction.
4. Motivate and develop the subordinates at all levels of hierarchy. To procure works in the Zone.
5. To conduct technical inspection of the work of the units.
6. Liaisoning with client/State Govt. and other bodies at appropriate levels.

(B) RBG/SBG/Zonal Finance In-charges

1. Overall In-charge of Finance Section of the Zone. All financial matter/decisions are required to be taken with the concurrence of Zonal Finance In-charge.
2. Compliance of statutory provision in the area of tax/levy/cess and industrial law.
3. Compliance of contractual terms and conditions with the contractors, consultants and other vendors and apprising/advising RBG/SBG/Zonal Heads/HO on these issues.
4. Maintaining all financial records/data, Books of accounts, returns and reports, approvals, Bills of vendors etc. in respect of all the projects under the RBG/SBG/Zone.
5. To observe functioning in RBG/SBG/Zones as per Delegation of Powers issued by the Corporate Office.

(C) Unit In-charges

1. Responsible for efficient management of the unit.
2. To organise site work efficiently and ensure timely completion of the work. Responsible for overall performance of the unit which includes execution of the work in accordance with the acceptable standards.

3. Responsible for 100% test check of each RA bill.
4. Maintaining all records of the work done, mandatory site registers, quality reports, approvals and bills of vendors etc. in respect of the project.
5. To ensure working in units as per Delegation of Powers issued by the Corporate Office.

History

NBCC was incorporated in 1960 as a wholly owned Government of India enterprise under the erstwhile Ministry of Works, Housing & Supply (MoWHS), which is now known as the Ministry of Housing and Urban Affairs (MoHUA).

In 1977, NBCC started its overseas operations.

In 2007, NBCC paid a dividend to the Government of India for the first time and since then, it has been paying a dividend every year. In the year 2008, the Department of Public Enterprises of the Ministry of Heavy Industries and Public Enterprises, through its office memorandum No. 9(8)/2008-GM dated 3 October 2008 accorded the approval of the Ministry of Housing and Urban Affairs upgrading NBCC from a Schedule "B" public sector enterprise to a Schedule "A" public sector enterprise. Subsequently, on 14 October 2008, the NBCC was granted Schedule "A" PSU status.

NBCC launched an IPO in April 2012 and was listed in BSE and NSE. In September 2012, NBCC was granted the Mini Ratna- I status by the Government of India.

The Government of India granted the status of a 'Navratna Company' to NBCC with effect from 23 June 2014. The status of a 'Navratna PSE' made NBCC eligible to invest up to ₹ 1,000 crore without the requirement of explicit government approval.

In October 2014, NBCC set up its wholly owned subsidiary NBCC Services Limited (NSL). In 2018, NBCC's order book had projects worth Rs 800 Billion.

Business segments

The Business Model of NBCC is categorised into three domains. They are project management consultancy (PMC), Engineering Procurement and Construction (EPC) and Real Estate Development.

- **Project Management Consultancy (PMC):** NBCC majorly works as a consultant on projects from concept stage to completion and maintenance. The company earns 93% of its revenue through consultation fees paid by the government body responsible for the project.
- **Engineering Procurement and Construction (EPC):** NBCC constructs cooling towers, chimneys, coal plants and ESIC hospitals through EPC services by doing feasibility studies, procurement, construction, designs and conceptualisation among others. The public sector behemoth acts as an EPC agency and also engages with various government departments for project clearances. EPC revenues are a minuscule percentage of company's trade.
- **Real Estate Development:** NBCC started real estate development in 1988. As of March 2019, it has been working as a land management agency for 10 CPSE's which include, HMT Watches, Hindustan Cables, Indian Drugs and Pharmaceuticals Ltd to create cost effective housing projects.

Revenue generation/redevelopment model: NBCC has been focusing on self-sustaining revenue generation model by taking up redevelopment of residential apartments for government employees and railway stations. It commercially develops the adjoining land parcels in the vicinity of the projects and makes it entirely self-sustainable. The major projects executed through this model are the GPRA colonies at New Moti Bag and East Kidwai Nagar, New Delhi.

Overseas Operations

In 1977, NBCC started working on international construction and infrastructure projects in the Middle East and African countries. The company has been engaged in the construction of National Prison Academy in Maldives, Supreme Court building and Social Housing project in Mauritius, Mahatma Gandhi International Convention Centres in 9 African countries and the India Pavilion at the Expo 2020.

Subsidiaries and Joint Ventures

NBCC has formed subsidiaries and Joint Ventures for construction and and infrastructure projects in India and abroad.

- NBCC Services Limited

- NBCC Gulf LLC
- NBCC Engineering & Consultancy Ltd.
- Hindustan Steel Works Construction Ltd
- Real Estate Development & Construction Corporation of Rajasthan Ltd.
- NBCC Environment Engineering Limited
- NBCC International Limited
- Hospital Services Consultancy Corporation Limited

Projects

National

- Indo-Bangladesh/Indo-Pak border fencing works
- 1200 bedded hospital and medical college at Guwahati, Assam
- Twin Tower World Trade Centre at Guwahati, Assam
- Hospitals for ESIC all across the country
- Solid Waste Management projects in 8 Airfield towns in India
- Bhubaneshwar and Mysore Airports
- NBCC Green View, Sector 37-D, Gurgaon
- VIBGYOR Towers, Kolkata- 876 flats/8 towers Residential Real Estate project
- NBCC Plaza, Sachet, New Delhi- Commercial Real Estate project
- LEED certified Green Building project named Indian Institute of Corporate Affairs (IICA) of the Ministry of Corporate Affairs at Mansard, Haryana
- Headquarter buildings for NIA, CBI, WHO in Delhi
- Redevelopment of 10 railway stations
- Construction of IITs, AIIMS and IIMs
- Baraka Super Thermal Power Project chimney for NTPC in West Bengal
- Constructions of two chimneys for NTPC at Bar, Bihar

Overseas

- Water Treatment Plant at Kirkuk, Iraq
- Birr Hospital in Nepal

- Construction, furnishing and equipping of 200 bedded Indira Gandhi Memorial Medical Hospital at Male, Maldives
- 48 km Kolhapur Mahakali Highway Project, Nepal
- Baghdad University
- Museum and Library Building, Hetaera, Nepal
- 1000 Houses at Bane Walled and 432 houses at Ghats, Libya
- Runway and Terminal building at Ghats and Bark Airport, Libya
- Construction of 774 housing units of Darwin, Dahmer, Yemen
- Project Management Consultancy for 3600 housing units at Meer Project in Turkey
- Hotel Nineveh Oberoi at Mosul, Baghdad.

Sustainable construction

NBCC has adopted a policy to incorporate sustainable green features into its projects. The features include Zero waste, Dual piping, Rainwater harvesting, Solar energy, smart electricity metering, and LED/energy efficient fixtures.[35] The projects undertaken by the company conform to Green Building norms. The company makes use of environment friendly techniques and materials such as steel structures, modular construction, pre-cast, pre-fab components and light weight concrete slabs.

The company also ensures strict compliance with the guidelines to curb air and water pollution at its project sites in its bid to contribute towards a safer environment.

Financial performance

- NBCC's total income stood at INR 10151.37 Cr in 2018-19.
- In the same period (2018–19) profit after tax stands at INR 391.64 Cr.
- Order pipeline of INR 75,000 cr approx.
- Net Worth: INR 1508.41 Cr.

National Mineral Development Corporation

Jump to navigationJump to search

This article **needs additional citations for verification**. Please help improve this article by adding citations to reliable sources. Unsourced material may be challenged and removed.

Find sources: "National Mineral Development Corporation" – news · newspapers · books · scholar · JSTOR *(June 2013) (Learn how and when to remove this template message)*

NMDC Limited

Formerly	National Mineral Development Corporation
Type	Public Sector Undertaking
Traded as	NSE: NMDC BSE: 526371
Industry	Mining
Founded	1958
Headquarters	Hyderabad, Telangana
Key people	Sumit Deb (Chairman & MD)

Products	Iron ore, copper, rock phosphate, limestone, dolomite, gypsum, bentonite, magnesite, diamond, tin, tungsten, graphite, and beach sands
Revenue	▼₹11,699.22 crore (US$1.6 billion) (2020)
Operating income	▼₹6,133.36 crore (US$860 million) (2020)
Net income	▼₹3,619.12 crore (US$510 million) (2020)
Total assets	▲₹31,143.94 crore (US$4.4 billion) (2020)
Total equity	▲₹27,533.95 crore (US$3.9 billion) (2020)
Owner	Government of India (69.65%)
Number of employees	5,887 (March 2019)
Website	www.nmdc.co.in

NMDC Limited, (formerly National Mineral Development Corporation), is an Indian public sector mineral producer. It is 69.65% owned by the Government of India, under the administrative control of the Ministry of Steel.

It is involved in the exploration of iron ore, copper, rock phosphate, limestone, dolomite, gypsum, bentonite, magnesite, diamond, tin, tungsten, graphite, etc.

It is India's largest iron ore producer and exporter, producing more than 35 million tonnes of iron ore from three mechanised mines in Chhattisgarh and Karnataka. It also operates the only mechanised diamond mine in the country at Panna in Madhya Pradesh.

Operating mines

- Bailadila Iron Ore Mine, Kirandul Complex, South Bastar district, Dantewada (C.G.)
- Bailadila Iron Ore Mine, Bacheli Complex, South Bastar district, Dantewada (C.G.)
- Donimalai Iron Ore Mine, Donimalai, Bellary district, Karnataka (at December 2019 suspended for over a year due to a royalty dispute)[6]
- Diamond Mining Project, Majhgawan, Panna (M.P.)

NMDC Ltd. is diversified into other raw materials for the steel industry such as low silica limestone. Production of dead burnt magnesite and further value addition is under study through its subsidiary J K Mineral Development Corporation Limited.

NMDC Ltd. has taken over a silica sand mining and beneficiation project from Uttar Pradesh State Mineral Development Corporation Ltd. The plant is designed to produce beneficiated high purity silica sand to a capacity of 300,000 tonnes per year as the raw material for production of float/sheet glass.

A memorandum of understanding has been signed between NMDC, Indian Rare Earths Limited, (IRE) and Andhra Pradesh Mineral Development Corporation to establish a joint venture for the development of Bheemunipatnam Beach Sand. The project envisages mining of beach sands, setting up of mineral separation plant for ilmenite concentrate and a downstream value addition plant for conversion of ilmenite into synthetic rutile/TiO_2 slag/TiO_2 pigment with pig iron as by-product.

Nagarnar Steel Plant

NMDC set up a 3 MTPA capacity Greenfield Nagarnar Steel Plant based on HiSmelt technology, 16 km from Jagdalpur in Chhattisgarh state, with an estimated outlay of ₹ 20000 crore.

A pure-play miner, NMDC had in 2009–10 conceived the Nagarnar steel plant with the intention of moving up the value chain and diversifying its portfolio. The idea was also to hedge itself against the vagaries of iron ore prices.

The plant site is around 16 km from Jagdalpur and 6 km from the Odisha–Chhattishgarh border. The nearest railway station is Amaguda (around 2 km). The site is located on National Highway NH 30. The nearby airports are Jagdalpur, Raipur & Vishakhapatnam and the nearest seaport is Vishakhapatnam located at a distance of approx 325 km. The nearest river is Indravati, local distance of 3 km.

Listings and shareholding

The equity shares of NMDC are listed on the Bombay Stock Exchange and the National Stock Exchange of India.

As of February 2020, the Government of India held a 69.65% equity in NMDC. 225,339 individual shareholders hold approximately 3.79% of its shares. The balance is held by insurance companies (14.31%), foreign institutional investors (5.78%), mutual funds (4.42%), and banks (1.96%). Life Insurance Corporation of India is the largest non-promoter shareholder in the company with a 12.89% shareholding.

International

In Australia, Legacy Iron Ore, a majority-owned NMDC company, **holds majority stakes in gold and iron ore projects in Western Australia.**

NMDC Limited was awarded the Corporate Social Responsibility Award Global Metals Award 2018 in the Corporate Social Responsibility category in London, the first time since inception that an Indian company received the award.

NLC India Limited

INDIA

CREATING WEALTH
FOR WELLBEING

NLC India's Corporate Office

Type	Public Sector Undertaking
Traded as	BSE: 513683 NSE: NLCINDIA
Industry	Mining and Electric utility
Founded	1956
Headquarters	Neyveli, Tamil Nadu, India
Products	Lignite and Electric power
Revenue	▲ ₹11,592.70 crore (US$1.6 billion) (2020)
Operating income	▲ ₹2,345.11 crore (US$330 million) (2020)
Net income	▼ ₹1,441.37 crore (US$200 million) (2020)
Total assets	▲ ₹53,488.13 crore (US$7.5 billion) (2020)
Total equity	▲ ₹12,905.13 crore (US$1.8 billion) (2020)
Owner	Government of India (79.20%)
Number of employees	12,675 (as on 31.01.2020)

NLC India Limited (NLC) (formerly Neyveli Lignite Corporation Limited) is a 'Navratna' government of India Company in the fossil fuel mining sector in India and thermal power generation. It annually produces about 30 million tonnes of Lignite from opencast mines at Neyveli in the state of Tamil Nadu in southern India and at Barsingsar in Bikaner district of Rajasthan state. The lignite is used at pithead thermal power stations of 3640 MW installed capacity to produce electricity. Its joint venture has a 1000 MW thermal power station using coal. Lately, it has diversified into renewable energy production and installed 1404 MW solar power plant to produce electricity from photovoltaic (PV) cells and 51 MW electricity from windmills.

It was incorporated in 1956 and was wholly owned by the Government of India. A small portion of its stock was sold to the public to list its shares on stock exchanges where its shares are traded. It is under the administrative control of Ministry of Coal.

History

Lignite Deposit was a chance finding when some 'brown substance' gushed out with water in Rao Bahadur M. Jambulingam Mudaliar's 620 acre own farm artesian well during 1934. He acted swiftly and contacted the then British Raj, which sent Geologists to Neyveli. It was later identified as 'Lignite'. He generously extended substantial portion of the sprawling land-bank for soil exploration. Through his effort and donated his 620 acres land to the Madras Government.

NLCIL has been a forerunner in the country in the energy sector for 62 years, contributing a lion's share in lignite production and significant share in thermal power generation. It was inaugurated by the first Prime Minister Jawaharlal Nehru in 1956.

NLCIL is a Navratna Government of India Enterprise. A pioneer in the energy sector, NLCIL operates four opencast lignite mines of a total capacity of 30.6 million tonnes Per Annum (MTPA) at Neyveli and Barsingsar, Rajasthan, Six lignite based pithead Thermal Power Stations with an aggregate capacity of 3640 MW – at Neyveli and Barsingsar and a 1000 MW Coal based Thermal Power Station at Thoothukudi, Tamil Nadu through its subsidiary company, NLC Tamil Nadu Power Limited (NTPL), a joint venture between NLCIL and TANGEDCO (equity participation in the ratio of 89:11). NLCIL recently commissioned a 1x500 MW unit at Neyveli which is also Asia's largest **lignite** fired boiler.

NLCIL has also forayed into renewable energy sector with commissioning of a 141 MW Solar Photo Voltaic Power Plant including 1 MW Roof-top Project at Neyveli and a 51 MW Wind Energy Plant at Kazhuneerkulam Village of Tirunelveli district in Tamil Nadu. The Company is also setting up 1209 MW Solar Power Projects at Tirunelveli, Virudhunagar and Ramanathapuram districts of Tamil Nadu, of which, 300 MW have been commissioned. NLC is aiming to achieve a total Renewable energy capacity of 4251 MW.

NLCIL has big dreams to become a 20000+ MW company by 2025. Towards realising this dream, NLC is already on expansion mode. Works are under progress for the Lignite based Neyveli New Thermal Power Plant (1000 MW), Bithnok TPS and Barsingsar TPS Expansion (each 250 MW). Further, NLC, jointly with the Uttar Pradesh Rajya Vidyut Utpadan Nigam Limited (UPRVUNL), is setting up a 3x660 MW Coal based Thermal Power Plant at Ghatampur in Uttar Pradesh, through its subsidiary company Neyveli Uttar Pradesh Power Limited (NUPPL) (equity participation in the ratio of 51:49). Apart from the above, the addition of Thermal Capacity to the tune of 6040 MW by way of installation of new plants and acquisition of Power Assets to the tune of 3000 MW is in the pipeline.

Not just Mining and Power Generation, NLCIL has contributed significantly to the Socio-Economic development for more than half a century.

The Business portfolio of the company is as under:

Chronology of events

Year	*Event*
1828	Occurrence of "PEAT" a low calorific fuel of coal family near Point Calimere is reported to the then Madras Government, by the sub-collector of Thanjavur Mr. Nelson.
1870	Peat bogs found in Nilgiris (Peat is considered to be the first stage in the formation of Coal from vegetable matter accumulating in swamps).
1877	Mr. W. King of the Geological Survey of India takes up a study of artesian wells around Pondicherry. He comes across a carbonaceous strata.
1884	Mr.Poilay, a French Engineer, encounters a Lignite seam in a bore hole at Bahoor, the then French territory. Further exploration along the belt indicates possible Lignite deposits at Udharamanickam, Aranganur, and Kanniakoil, near Cuddalore. Lignite deposits are indicated at Kasargod and the Collector of South Kanara reports it to the Board of Revenue.
1934	Industries Department of the then Government of Madras drills bore holes for tapping artesian water in the neighbourhood of Neyveli. Lignite particles encountered are taken as "black - clay" by unlettered workmen engaged in drilling.
1935	Borewells sunk in Jambulinga Mudaliyar's land in Neyveli and the black particles gushing forth attract the attention of camping Geologists engaged in some other mission in the Neyveli Vriddhachalam area.
1937-1938	Samples of the black substance taken from the above form well sent to the Government of Madras for analysis.
1941	M/s. Binny & Co., Madras put down four or five bore holes at Aziz Nagar, near Neyveli. Two of them show evidence of Lignite deposits, but further work is given up for want of casing pipes and drilling equipment.
1943-1946	The Geological Survey of India starts drilling operations near Neyveli. Preliminary investigations indicate the existence of Lignite to the extent of about 500 tonnes in that area.
1947	Mr.H.K. Ghose, Geologist and Mining Engineer deputed by the Government of India arrives in Neyveli and starts his operations.

1948	The first bore holes sunk by Mr. Ghose have to be abandoned because of waterlogging and sand - beds. The third one "September 1951" yields samples of Lignite.
1949	Mr. Ghose draws an experimental open-cut plan and calls for tenders to start excavation.
1951	Sinking 175 borewells in a cluster punctuating the chosen area, Mr. Ghose proves the existence of about 2000 Million tonnes of Lignite reserves in the area. State Government's Industries and Commerce Department also sinks over 150 borewells South of Vriddhachalam. Mr. Paul Eyrich, a Mining Engineer, is deputed by the Bureau of Mines, United States of America, to assist the Government of Madras under point four programme to determine the Engineering and Economic aspects of Lignite Mining in Neyveli. Upon his recommendation, the US Government sponsors a study on the subject under the direction of Mr. V.F. Parry.
1952	The High Power Committee for Lignite Mining recommends the Pilot Quarry project.
1953	Pilot Quarry being commissioned by Dr. U. Krishna Rao, Minister for Industries, Madras Government.
1954	Nehru's visit to the pilot Quarry. Government of India's Committee comprising Mr. C.V. Narasimhan, ICS, Mr. A.C. Guha and Mr. A. Lahiri inspect the Pilot Quarry and submit a report to the Government. Under the Colombo Plan, services of the UK firm PDTS (M/s. Powell Duffryn Technical Services Limited) are availed of for a Project report.
1955	Neyveli Lignite project's affairs, hitherto managed by the State Government, get passed on to the Central Government with full Financial responsibility. Mr. T.M.S. Mani, ICS, Secretary, Department of Industries, Labour and Co-operation, takes over as the Chief Executive of the project.
1956	Formation of NLC as a Corporate body. NLC is born as a Government-sponsored commercial concern.

Power projects

NLC India has five pithead Thermal Power Stations with an aggregate capacity of 4240 MW. Further, NLC India has so far installed 51 Wind Turbine Generators of capacity 1.50 MW each and also commissioned 140 MW Solar Photo Voltaic Power plant in Neyveli, resulting in an overall power generating capacity of 4431 MW (excl. JVs).

Power Plants	***Capacity (MW)***
TPS – I	600
TPS – II	1470
TPS - I Expansion	420

Barsingsar TPS	250
TPS - II Expansion	500
Wind Power Plant	51
Solar Power Plant	1404
NTPL	1000
NNTPP	1000
TOTAL	6695

Thermal Power Station I

The 600 MW Neyveli Thermal Power Station-I in which the first unit was synchronised in May 1962 and the last unit in September 1970 consists of six units of 50 MW each and three units of 100 MW each. The Power generated from Thermal Power Station-I after meeting NLC's requirements is supplied to TANGEDCO, Tamil Nadu which is the sole beneficiary. Due to the aging of the equipments / high-pressure parts, the Life extension programme has been approved by GOI in March 1992 and was completed in March 1999 thus extending the life by 15 years. Given the high grid demand in this region, this power station is being operated after conducting the Residual Life Assessment (RLA) study. GOI has sanctioned a 2x500 MW Power Project (Neyveli New Thermal Power Plant – NNTPS) in June 2011 as a replacement for existing TPS-I.

Thermal Power Station II

The 1470 MW Second Thermal Power Station consists of 7 units of 210 MW each. In February 1978, the Government of India sanctioned the Second Thermal Power Station of 630 MW capacity (3 × 210 MW) and in Feb. 1983, the Government of India sanctioned the Second Thermal Power Station Expansion from 630 MW to 1470 MW with addition of 4 units of 210 MW each. The first 210 MW unit was synchronised in March 1986 and the last unit (Unit-VII) was synchronised in June 1993. The power generated from Second Thermal Power Station after meeting the needs of Second Mine is shared by the Southern States viz., Tamil Nadu, Kerala, Karnataka, Andhra Pradesh and Union Territory of Pondicherry.

Thermal Power Station I - Expansion

Thermal Power Station-I has been expanded (2 x 210 MW) using the lignite available from Mine-I Expansion. The scheme, TPS I Expansion, was sanctioned by the Government of India in February 1996. Unit-I was synchronised in October 2002 and Unit-II in July 2003. The power generated from this Thermal Power Station, after meeting the internal requirements, is shared by the Southern States viz., Tamil Nadu, Kerala, Karnataka, and Union Territory of Pondicherry.

Barsingsar Thermal Power Station

The Government of India sanctioned the Barsingsar Thermal Power Station 250 MW (2 × 125 MW) in October 2004. The units were commissioned in December 2011 and in January 2012. The power generated from this Thermal Power Station after meeting internal requirements is shared by the DISCOMS of the state of Rajasthan.

Thermal Power Station II - 1st Expansion

This Project is consisting of two units of 250 MW capacity each. Unit-II attained commercial operation in April 2015 and Unit-I in July 2015. The lignite requirement is met through expansion of Mine-II. The steam generators of this project employ eco-friendly Circulating Fluidised Bed Combustion (CFBC) technology. This technology has been adopted for 250 MW Capacity units for the first time in India.

Gallery

- **Mining Projects**

NLC has four open cast lignite mines, namely, Mine I, Mine II, Mine IA and Barsingsar Mine. The lignite mined out is used as fuel to the linked pithead power stations. Also, raw lignite is being sold to small scale industries to use it as fuel in their production activities.

Mines	Capacity (in MTPA)
Mine I	10.5
Mine I A	3.0
Mine II	15.0
Barsingsar Mine	2.1

Gallery

Mine I

Mine II

Mine IA

Joint venture projects

NLC Tamil Nadu Power Ltd. (NTPL) (2 x 500 MW)

NTPL (2 x 500 MW) Thermal Power Plant, Tuticorin, Tamil Nadu

NLC Tamil Nadu Power Limited (NTPL), is a joint venture company of NLC India Ltd (formerly known as NLC Ltd) and M/s TANGEDCO (Tamil Nadu Generation and Distribution Company), incorporated under the Company Act. The Equity participation between NLC and TANGEDCO is at the ratio of 89:11. GOI had issued sanction for the implementation of coal-based 2 × 500MW Thermal Power Project by NTPL at Tuticorin at an estimated cost of ₹ 4909.54 Cr. Unit 1 and Unit 2 has been declared for commercial operation w.e.f. 18 June 2015 and 29 August 2015. RCE – 2 for the project (Completion cost of the project) works out to ₹ 7293.48 Cr. (June – 15 base). Power Purchase Agreement has been signed with TANGEDCO, ESCOMs of Karnataka State, Puducherry Electricity Department, Kerala State Electricity Board and DISCOMs of Andhra Pradesh. Power evacuation from this project is being carried out by M/s Power Grid Corporation of India.NTPL has signed a fuel supply agreement with Mahanadhi Coal fields Limited for supply of 3.0 MTPA of coal and to meet the shortfall in the requirement, a contract has also been awarded on M/s. MSTC for the supply of imported coal.

Neyveli Uttar Pradesh Power Ltd. (NUPPL) (3 x 660 MW)

Neyveli Uttar Pradesh Power Limited (NUPPL) is a joint venture between NLC India and Uttar Pradesh Rajya Vidyut Utpadan Nigam Limited, for setting up of 3 x 660 MW power project at Ghatampur, Uttar Pradesh.

Upcoming Projects

Neyveli New Thermal Power Project (NNTPP) (2 × 500 MW)

The Neyveli New Thermal Power Project (2x500 MW) is being implemented at a capital cost of ₹ 5907.11 Cr as a replacement for the more than five decades old 600 MW Thermal Power Station I and adopts pulverised fuel firing technology. Consequent to re-tendering of Steam Generator package the Units are rescheduled to be commissioned in October 2017 and April 2018. LOA for Steam Generator package(NTA 1) and Turbo-Generator package (NTA 2) has been issued to M/s BHEL and detailed engineering activities, civil and mechanical erection works and supplies are in progress. LOA has also been issued for the Balance of Plant Package and the engineering and civil works, supplies and erection are in progress.

Expansion of Mine I-A

In order to meet the additional requirement of lignite arising out of implementation of 1000 MW Neyveli New Thermal Power Project at Neyveli, expansion of Mine-IA is being implemented, which would result in raising the Mine IA capacity by 4 MTPA. Acquisition of required land has been taken up with government. Ministry of Coal has accorded approval for mining expansion plan of MINE 1A.

Wind Power Plant (51 MW)

NLC India is implementing Wind Power farm of capacity 51 MW at Kazhuneerkulam in the State of Tamil Nadu at an estimated cost of ₹ 347.14 Cr. M/s LeitwindShriram Manufacturing Limited is the implementing agency and so far 29 Nos. of Wind Turbine Generators (WTG) have been commissioned and the balance 5 Nos. are expected to be commissioned during the year 2016. Power Purchase Agreement has been signed with TANGEDCO.

Neyveli Solar Power Project (2 × 65 MW)

NLC India is setting up 130 MW Solar power project at Neyveli, Tamil Nadu. The project is implemented through EPC route and scheduled to be commissioned in 2016-17. M/s BHEL and M/s Jakson bagged the contract and LOA has been issued. Power Purchase Agreement has been signed with TANGEDCO.

Bithnok Thermal Power Project (250 MW)

Bithnok Thermal Power Project (250 MW) with the linked lignite mine of 2.25 MTPA capacity at Bithnok in the State of Rajasthan is being set up at an aggregate estimated cost of ₹ 2709.93 Cr. Power Purchase Agreement has been signed with Rajasthan DISCOMs. Agreement for supply of 25 cusecs of water from IGNP canal has been entered into. Government of Rajasthan (GoR) has issued award for acquisition of 1175.87 hectares of private land in Bithnok and 1863.184 Ha of Government land will be diverted to project by GoR after takeover of private land. The project is proposed to be implemented through Engineering, Procurement and Commissioning (EPC) contract mode and is expected to be commissioned during the year 2020. Ministry of Coal has accorded approval for revised mining plan in June 2015. EOI short listing is completed and techno-commercial evaluation is in progress.

Barsingsar Thermal Power Project Extension (250 MW)

A lignite based Thermal Power Plant with a capacity of 250 MW as an extension of the existing power plant at Barsingsar is being set up. The fuel requirement for the above power plant is to be met from linked Hadla Mine of 1.9 MTPA and the existing Barsingsar Mine. The aggregate estimated cost of the project is ₹ 2635.04 Crores. All statutory clearances have been obtained. Government of Rajasthan has allocated Mining Lease area of 15.66 Sq. km. The project is proposed to be implemented through Engineering, Procurement and Commissioning (EPC) route and is expected to be commissioned during the year 2020. EOI short listing is completed and techno-commercial evaluation is in progress.

Sirkazhi Thermal Power Project (3960 MW)

It is proposed to set up a coal based thermal power project with an overall capacity of 3960 MW, in two phases, at Sirkazhi in the coastal district of Nagapattinam, in the State of Tamil Nadu Advance Action Proposal at a cost of ₹ 56.52 Cr for taking up pre-project activities is in progress. NLCI has identified Thirumullaivasal as the site for locating the power plant. Feasibility report is under preparation. Action has been initiated for floating tender for preparation of CRZ map for the project. Application for land acquisition has been submitted to Government of Tamil Nadu for issue of administrative sanction for acquisition of land for this project. Preparations of EIA/EMP report, DPR for captive coal jetty are in process. Change in configuration to 5 x 800 MW using super critical technology is under active consideration.

Thermal Power Station II - 2nd Expansion (2 x 660 MW)

It is proposed to increase the power generating capacity by adding another 1320 MW thermal power plant as the second expansion to the existing TPS-II at Neyveli. A new mine, Mine-III of capacity of 11.5 MTPA is proposed to be set up to exploit the mineable lignite reserves of about 380 MT available in the south of the existing Mine-II to meet the fuel requirement of the proposed thermal power plant. Advanced Action Proposals (AAP) of ₹ 7.05 Cr for Mine-III and ₹ 1.80 Cr for TPS-II Second Expansion for taking up phase-I pre-project activities were approved. Action has been initiated to enter into Power Purchase Agreement with DISCOMs of Southern States. PPA has been signed with TANGEDCO, Kerala SEB, Puducherry, Government of Andhra Pradesh, and Government of Telangana.

Mine II - Augmentation

It is proposed to augment Mine-II from the present capacity of 15.0 MTPA to 18.75 MTPA, in order to meet the lignite requirements of TPS-II including Expansion for operating at a higher Plant Load Factor (PLF).

Talabira II and III, OCP (20 MTPA) and Talabira Thermal Power Plant (3200 MW)

The government has allotted Talabira-II and III coal blocks in Odisha to power NLC India Limited which is looking to ramp up coal-based electricity generation capacity.

NLC plans to have 19,000 MW capacity by 2025; projects to generate 6,000 MW from coal and 2,500 MW from lignite are already underway.

NLC is expediting to set up a pit head coal based power project in Odisha with the capacity of 3,200 MW. The power plant will entail an estimated investment of ₹ 17000 crore, and is to be built at Tareikela near Jharsuguda in the western part of Odisha.

The said power plant would be linked to Talabira II and III coal block in Sambalpur and Jharsuguda District which has a mineable reserve of 553.98 Million Metric Tons. The annual capacity of the mine is 20 MTPA.

Currently, the mine is being developed by NLC India and its mine operator and developer, M/s Talabira Odisha Mining Private Limited, a subsidiary of Adani Enterprises Limited.

Pachwara south coal block 10 MTPA in Jharkhand

Oil India

This article is about the hydrocarbon exploration and production company. For the company involved in refining, pipeline transportation and marketing of petroleum products, see Indian Oil Corporation.

This article **needs additional citations for verification**. Please help improve this article by adding citations to reliable sources. Unsourced material may be challenged and removed.
Find sources: "Oil India" – news · newspapers · books · scholar · JSTOR *(June 2015) (Learn how and when to remove this template message)*

Oil India Limited

ऑयल इंडिया लिमिटेड

Oil India Limited

Type	Public Sector Undertaking
Traded as	NSE: OIL BSE: 533106
Industry	Oil and Gas
Founded	18 February 1959
Headquarters	Noida (headquarters) Duliajan (registered office)
Key people	Sushil Chandra Mishra (Chairman & MD)
Products	Petroleum Natural gas Petrochemicals
Revenue	▼₹12,128.52 crore (US$1.7 billion) (2020) [1]
Operating income	▼₹2,618.9 crore (US$370 million) (2020)
Net income	▼₹2,584.06 crore (US$360 million) (2020)
Total assets	▼₹42,841.39 crore (US$6.0 billion) (2020)
Total equity	▼₹24,386.67 crore (US$3.4 billion) (2020)
Owner	Government of India (61.64%)
Number of employees	7,097 (March 2019)
Website	www.oil-india.com

Oil India Limited (OIL) is the second largest hydrocarbon exploration and production Indian public sector company with its operational headquarters in Duliajan, Assam, India. The company is a state-owned Navratna under the administrative control of India's Ministry of Petroleum and Natural Gas with its corporate offices in Noida in the New Delhi-NCR region.

OIL is engaged in the business of exploration, development and production of crude oil and natural gas, transportation of crude oil and production of liquid petroleum gas. The company's history spans the discovery of crude oil in the far east of India at Digboi and Baghjan, Assam in 1889 to its present status as a fully integrated upstream petroleum company.

Exploration and production

Oil India Limited was formed by the Burmah Oil Company Limited as its subsidiary in India 1887 to explore in the Assam Basin, India (Corley, T A B, 1983, The History of the Burmah Oil Company, 1886-1983). Staff at the Burmah Oil Company Limited had heard from a geologist with the colonial British Indian Geological Survey, Thomas Oldham, that oil was found on the feet of elephants that were being used as beasts of burden in the vicinity of the Digboi village (Arun Metrie, pers. comm., former Burmah Oil economist, 1988). The oil on the elephants' feet was traced to the Digboi area, where a surface fold (anticline in geological parlance) had formed a broad hill. A successful technique for exploration for hydrocarbons at the time was drilling beneath seeps on anticlines (Thornton, S E, 2015, the history of Oil Exploration in the Union of Myanmar, Paper No. 10807), so Oil India drilled beneath the Digboi seeps and found a giant oil field. Several other oil fields were subsequently found by Oil India Limited in what became India's first oil production.

Recoverable oil reserves. As of 2014 the company produced 3.466 MMT of crude oil, 2625.81 million cubic metres at standard conditions of natural gas and 46,640 tonnes of LPG. Most of this was produced from its traditionally rich oil and gas fields concentrated in the Northeastern part of India and contribute around 80% of total oil and gas produced in the region. The search for newer avenues has seen OIL spreading out its operations in onshore / offshore Odisha and Andaman, Cauvery offshore, Tamil Nadu, Arabian Sea, deserts of Rajasthan, onshore Andhra Pradesh, riverbeds of Brahmaputra and logistically difficult hilly terrains of the Indian state Mizoram and Arunachal Pradesh. In Rajasthan, OIL discovered gas in 1988, heavy oil / bitumen in 1991 and started production of gas in 1996. The company has accumulated over a hundred years of experience in the field of oil and gas production, since the discovery of Digboi oilfield in 1889.

The company has over 100,000 square kilometres (39,000 sq mi) of licenced areas for oil and gas exploration. It has emerged as a consistently profitable International company] and present in Libya, Gabon, Nigeria, Sudan, Venezuela, Mozambique, Yemen, Iran, Bangladesh and United States. OIL has recently emerged in the offshore giant gas-field project of Mozambique and also made discovery of oil and gas in Gabon as an Operator and Libya as non-operator. OIL acquired Shale oil asset in United States during 2012.

In recent years, OIL has stepped up exploration and production activities significantly in north-eastern India. OIL has set up its NEF (North East Frontier) project to intensify its exploration activities in the frontier areas in North East, which are logistically very difficult and geologically complex. Presently, exploration activities are in progress along the Trust Belt areas of Arunachal, Assam including Mizoram. The Company operates a crude oil pipeline from Duliajan to Barauni, in Bihar.

History

Oil India was founded on 18 February 1959, with its registered office in Duliajan, Assam, as a privately-held oil exploration company. Burmah Oil Company originally held two-thirds of the stock and the Government of India (via the Office of the President) held the rest. In the spring of 1961 the company became publicly listed, and later that year the Government of India acquired 50% ownership interest. In 1981, the Government of India acquired 100% of the equity interest in the company. The company was created to exploit the oil fields of Naharkatiya and Moran in north-eastern India, which had then been just recently discovered.

In 1961, construction of the company's first gas-powered power plant was completed in Duliajan, Assam. In 1962, a 401 km (16-inch diameter) pipeline from Duliajan to Guwahati was completed. The following year, a 756 km (14-inch diameter) extension to the pipeline from Guwahati to Barauni in Bihar was completed.

A 1,157-kilometre (719 mi) long fully automated telemetric pipeline with 212 kilometres (132 mi) of looping and a total capacity to transport over 6 million tonnes per year remains the lifeline of the company. Commissioned in 1962, the double skinned crude oil pipeline traverses 78 rivers including the Brahmaputra River as it meanders through paddy fields, forests and swamps. There are 11 pumping stations, 18 repeater stations and two terminals at

Numaligarh and Rongapani in Udalguri district. The engines that drive the giant pumps along the pipeline have more than two hundred thousand hours of service and established a world record of machine hours.

OIL completed the construction of a 660-kilometre (410 mi) pipeline from Numaligarh to Siliguri in November 2007. The company also sells its gas to different customers in Assam: Brahmaputra Valley Fertiliser Corporation Limited (BVFCL), ASEB, NEEPCO, Indian Oil Corporation's retail Assam Oil Division, and APL as well as to the Rajasthan Rajya Vidyut Utpadan Nigam formerly part of the Rajasthan State Electricity Board (RSEB). It also produces liquefied petroleum gas (LPG) at its plant in Duliajan, Assam.

Management

Chairman and Managing Directors (CMDs)

- 1992 to 1995 - Bikash Chandra Bora
- May 2002 to 28 February 2006 - Ranjit Kumar Dutta
- 14 March 2006 to 1 December 2008 - Mulkh Raj Pasrija
- 1 December 2008 to April 2012 - Nayan Mani Borah
- May 2012 to 30 June 2015 - S. K. Srivastava
- 1 July 2015 to 17 July 2016 - vacant
- 18 July 2016 to 30 September 2019 - Utpal Bora
- 1 October 2019 to present - Sushil Chandra Mishra

International Operations

OIL's overseas E & P portfolio consists of 17 Blocks spread over 10 countries: Libya, Gabon, Nigeria, Yemen, Venezuela, USA, Mozambique, Myanmar, Bangladesh and Russia. In addition to the above, OIL has 10% PI in 741 km long Multiproduct pipeline construction and operation project in Sudan which was completed in 2005.

Subsidiaries

Oil India Limited carries out operations through a total of five subsidiaries, namely, OIIL (Oil Indian International Limited), Oil India International BV, Oil India Sweden AB, Oil Indian (USA) Inc and OIL Cyprus.[16]

During 2016-17

OIL along with Indian Consortium partners IOCL and BPRL acquired two producing assets in Russia - 23.9% stake in Vankorneft, Russia and 29.9% stake in Taas-Yuryakh, Russia. These assets are held through OIL's WOS Oil India International Pte. Ltd. incorporated in Singapore.

TYNGD is a producing asset with current production of 1.13 MMT and expected peak production of 5 MMT by 2021. It is one of the largest green fields located in Eastern Siberia. TYNGD is ramping up required infrastructure to meet peak production level.

Vankorneft has two licences - Vankor and North Vankor. It is a giant oil and gas producing field located in Eastern Siberia, and contributes to about 10% of Rosneft's entire oil production. The commercial agreements for sale of oil and gas are in place for the asset. Vankorneft started commercial production from 2009 and all infrastructure is in place.

In Licence-61 in Russia, the development and production activities are undergoing at present. OIL is taking an active role in the development activities and supporting the operator of the licence, M/s Petroneft Resources by providing expert opinions in selected areas.

In Venezuela, Carabobo Project where OIL has PI of 3.5%, the development activities in the field are under progress.

In the USA Liquid rich shale asset where OIL has 20% PI, OIL holds approx. 14172.75 net acres of the asset. Currently, OIL's share of daily production from this asset is around 350 barrels (56 cubic metres) per day of oil equivalent.

OIL together with OVL, has 10 percent participating interest (OIL 4%, OVL 6%) in the Mozambique block in the Area 1 Rovuma Field, the Initial development of Integrated Golfino-Atum (GA) Project. The Area 1 JV is presently working on Four elements, viz. (i) Legal and Contractual framework, (ii) Resettlement of the local community, (iii) Marketing of LNG, (iv) Project Financing, that must be sufficiently progressed before Operator Anadarko and the participants can determine economic viability and take Final Investment decision. The first production and revenue from the field is expected to be generated in fiscal year 2022/2023.

In Libya, in the block Area 95/96, OIL holds 25% PI and Sonatrach is the operator. The consortium signed an Interim Arrangement Agreement to continue in the block till May 2018.

In Gabon, Block SHAKTHI, a discovery has been made, which produced oil with gas.

In Nigeria, Based on the interpreted results, consortium decided to re-enter the (Discovery Well) and re-entry in the well is under progress now.

In Bangladesh, seismic acquisition and processing of acquired data is almost complete.

In Myanmar, the Consortium led by OIL has completed Geoscientific Studies.

OIL's overseas portfolio has contributed significantly to accretion of reserves and production of oil and Natural gas. During 2016-17, OIL's Crude Oil and Natural Gas Production for its proportionate share of stakes in the overseas producing assets stood at 0.9069 MMT and 352.99 million cubic metres at standard conditions respectively.

Power Finance Corporation Ltd.

Type	Public Sector Undertaking
Traded as	NSE: PFC BSE: 532810
Industry	Financial services
Genre	Financial Services Company
Founded	July 1986
Headquarters	New Delhi, India
Area Served	India

Key people	Ravinder Singh Dhillon IAS (Chairman & MD)
Products	Rupee Term Loan, Foreign Currency Loan, Short Term Loan
Services	Financial Consulting, Financial Products, Investment Banking, Loan Management, Linkage Management
Revenue	▲₹33,362.90 crore (US$4.7 billion) (2020)
Operating income	▲₹30,045.73 crore (US$4.2 billion) (2020)
Net income	▼₹5,655.14 crore (US$790 million) (2020)
Total assets	▲₹361,787.26 crore (US$51 billion) (2020)
Total equity	▲₹45,164.13 crore (US$6.3 billion) (2020)
Owner	Government of India (52.63%)
Number of employees	498 (March 2019)
Website	pfcindia.com

Power Finance Corporation Ltd. (P.F.C.) is an Indian financial institution. Established in 1986, it is the financial backbone of Indian Power Sector. PFC's Net worth as on 30 September 2018 is INR 383 billion. PFC is the 8th highest profit making CPSE as per the Department of Public Enterprises Survey for FY 2017–18. PFC is India's largest NBFC and also India's largest infrastructure finance company.

Initially wholly owned by the Government of India, the company issued an initial public offering in January, 2007. The issue was oversubscribed by over 76 times, which is one of the largest for an IPO of any Indian company. PFC is listed on the Bombay Stock Exchange (BSE) and the National Stock Exchange (NSE). It is also an ISO 9001:2000 certified company and enjoys the status of Navratna Company in India. On 6 December 2018, the Government of India approved PFC's takeover of REC. The acquisition transaction was completed on 28 March 2019 with PFC paying almost ₹ 14,500 Crs to the Govt. of India for the 52.63% stake.

Organisation structure

The corporation is headed by the chairman and managing director, who at present is Ravinder Singh Dhillon. The company has three wings, each headed by a Functional Director namely, Commercial Division, Projects Division and Finance & Financial Operations division. The Commercial Division looks after the credit appraisal and categorisation of borrower entities, power sector reforms, review and analysis. The Projects Division controls the operation in various states and project appraisal. Finance Division looks after the Fund Mobilisation and Disbursement. PFC is a lean organisation. The number of employees as on 31 March 2019 was around 500.

Borrowings

The major part of PFC's funds are raised through Rupee-denominated bonds. PFC bonds enjoy the highest credit rating in the Indian market and in international markets; they are rated at par with the Indian Sovereign rating. It also borrows short term and long term from various banks and other financial institutions. It has also raised external commercial borrowings (ECB) through private placement in US market. PFC is one of the institutions eligible for raising funds through capital gain tax bonds under section 54EC of the Income Tax Act, 1961.

Over the last two-three years PFC has focused on diversifying its borrowing portfolio by raising funds from international markets. In November 2017, PFC launched its main Green Bond issue for US$400 million, which witnessed the tightest ever spread for any Indian Issuer for its maiden 10-year issue. In the first quarter of financial year 2020, PFC has raised about US$1.3 billion from the international markets. Out of this US$1 billion was raised in June 2019, which was the first dual and largest USD bonds transaction for Govt owned Indian NBFC. This was also PFC's first borrowing from the international markets after the successful acquisition of REC Limited.

In 2017, PFC was granted approval by Ministry of Finance, Govt. of India, to raise funds under section 54EC of the Income Tax Act 1961. PFC was the first company to obtain such an approval post the budget announcement in February 2017. PFC has raised more than ₹ 1,000 Crs under these bonds since their launch in 2017.

Operations

Since its inception, PFC has been providing financial assistance to power projects across India including generation, transmission, distribution and RM&U projects. Recently, it has forayed into financing of other infrastructure projects which have backward linkages to the power sector like coal mine development, fuel transportation, oil and gas pipelines etc. The borrower profile includes State Electricity Boards, State sector power utilities, Central sector power utilities and Private sector companies. PFC is also the nodal agency for the implementation of the ambitious Ultra Mega Power Plants (UMPPs) and the R-APDRP programme of Govt. of India. The company also has the mechanism of rating different state Power Utilities on its performance.

Subsidiary and Associate Companies

PFC presently has ten subsidiary companies. PFC Consulting Ltd. (PFCCL) is a wholly owned subsidiary handling fee based services. The six other companies namely, Orissa Integrated Power Limited, Coastal Karnataka Power Limited, Coastal Tamil Nadu Power Limited, Coastal Maharashtra Power Limited, Jharkhand Integrated Power Limited and Akaltara Power Limited, are SPVs (Shell Companies) created for implementing the flagship Ultra Mega Power Projects. After purchase of the entire holding of Govt. of India in Rural Electrification Corporation Limited (REC) in FY 2018-19, REC has now become a subsidiary of PFC.

PFC is also one of the promoters in Energy Efficiency Services Limited (EESL), with NTPC, Powergrid and REC being the other promoters. EESL is currently implementing of world's largest energy efficiency portfolio and has been instrumental in energy savings of more than 50 billion kWh/year and estimated GHG reduction of more than 40 million tons CO_2/year.

Awards and recognitions

1.	MOU Excellence Award 2009-10	January, 2012
2.	KPMG-Infrastructure Today Award 2011	December, 2011
3.	Dainik Bhasker India Pride PSU Award 2011	October, 2011
4.	SCOPE Commendation Certificate 2009-10	April, 2011
5.	Global HR Excellence Awards 2011	February, 2011
6.	KPMG-Infrastructure Today Award 2008	December, 2008

7.	India Power Award 2008	November, 2008
8.	Golden Peacock Award 2007	September, 2007
9.	Navratna Company	June, 2007

Notes

1. ^ https://www.pfcindia.com/DocumentRepository/ckfinder/files/Investors/Annual_Reports/PFC%20AR%202018-19%20final.pdf
2. ^ PFC Investor Presentation Quarter 2 FY 2018–19
3. ^ "PFC's IPO over-subscribed 73 times - Economic Times". Economictimes.indiatimes.com. 7 February 2007. Retrieved 29 November 2012.
4. ^ Chennai Online, 5 Aug 2004 Archived 24 December 2009 at the Wayback Machine
5. ^ Singh, Sarita (6 December 2018). "Cabinet approves REC takeover by Power Finance Corporation". The Economic Times. Retrieved 30 May 2019.
6. ^ www.ETEnergyworld.com. "PFC appoints Ravindra Singh Dhillon as CMD from June 1 - ET EnergyWorld". ETEnergyworld.com. Retrieved 11 June 2020.
7. ^ About R-APDRP
8. ^ About R-APDRP from PFC website

Rashtriya Ispat Nigam

Rashtriya Ispat Nigam Limited

Type	Public Sector Undertaking
Industry	Steel Iron
Founded	18 February 1982
Headquarters	Visakhapatnam, India
Key people	Pradosh Kumar Rath (Chairman & MD)
Products	Wire rods, TMT Re-bars, rounds, squares, flats, angles, channels, Rail Wheels

Services	Steel production
Revenue	▲₹20,492.03 crore (US$2.9 billion) (2018-2019)[2]
Net income	▲₹96.71 crore (US$14 million) (2018-19)[2]
Total assets	▲₹35,201.31 crore (US$4.9 billion) (2018-19)
Total equity	▲₹7,352.28 crore (US$1.0 billion) (2018-19)
Owner	Government of India
Number of employees	17,574 (March 2019)
Subsidiaries	Eastern Investments Limited (EIL) The Orissa Minerals Development Company Limited (OMDC) The Bisra Stone Lime Company Limited (BSLC)
Website	www.vizagsteel.com

Rashtriya Ispat Nigam Ltd, (abbreviated as **RINL**), also known as *Vizag Steel,* is a public steel producer based in Visakhapatnam, India. Rashtriya Ispat Nigam Limited (RINL) is the corporate entity of Visakhapatnam Steel Plant (VSP), India's first shore-based integrated steel plant built with state-of-the-art technology. Visakhapatnam Steel Plant (VSP) is a 7.3 MTPA plant. It was commissioned in 1992 with a capacity of 3.0 MTPA of liquid steel. The company subsequently completed its capacity expansion to 6.3 MTPA in April 2015 and to 7.3 MTPA in December 2017. The company is having one subsidiary, viz. Eastern Investment Limited (EIL) with 51% shareholding, which in turn is having two subsidiaries, viz. M/s Orissa Mineral Development Company Ltd (OMDC) and M/s Bisra Stone Lime Company Ltd (BSLC). The company has a partnership in RINMOIL Ferro Alloys Private Limited and International Coal Ventures Limited in the form of Joint Ventures with 50% and 26.49% shareholding respectively.

RINL, with an exclusive product mix of longs, is the largest producer of "Bars and Rods" in the country with a market share of 9.5% in 2018–19 (Source: JPC) and has recorded an annual turnover of ₹ 20,844 crore (Prov.) in 2018–19. The products of RINL include Rebars, Wire Rods, Rounds, Structurals, Blooms & Billets, and Pig Iron and the company also markets the resultant by-products like coal chemicals (Ammonium Sulphate, Benzol products, etc.) and Slag. RINL products are known for its quality RINL is one of the major players in the country for Long Products having three Captive Mines and 25 Marketing Branches Pan India. Forged Wheel Plant is another unit of RINL being set up at Raebareli, Uttar Pradesh.

Location

The Steel plant is located in the southern part of Visakhapatnam city, Andhra Pradesh state of India. The company also has blast furnace grade Limestone captive mine at Jaggayyapeta (Krishna District), a captive mine for Dolomite at Madharam (Khammam), a manganese ore captive mine at Cheepurupalli (Vizianagaram). It also has a mining lease for river sand of river Champavathi.

History

Making the Impossible possible lies in man's determination and Sri Tenneti Viswanadham and T. Amrutha Rao (Ex. M.L.A, Tadikonda - Amaravathi 1978-83, "Ukku Satyagrahi" - "Visakha Ukku Andhrula Hakku") were two such personalities. The struggle of thousands of such personalities has paved a way for establishing such a big steel plant. The activities kicked off by appointing the site selection committee in June 1970 and subsequently committee report was approved for the site. In January 1971, then PM of India has laid the foundation stone. Consultants were appointed in February 1971 and feasibility reports were submitted in 1972. The first block of land was taken over in April 1974. M/s M.N. Dastur & Co was appointed as the consultant for preparing the detailed project report in April 1975, and in October 1977 they have submitted the report for 3.4 MTPA of liquid steel. With the government of erstwhile USSR's offer for assistance, a revised project concept was evolved. DPR for a plant capacity of 3.4 MTPA was prepared by Ms. M.N. Dastur & Co in November 1980. In February 1981 contract was signed with Soviet-Union for preparation of working drawings for coke ovens, blast furnace, and sinter plant. The blast furnace foundation was laid with first mass concreting in the project in January 1982. The construction of township also started.

RINL was wholly owned by the Government of India. In November 2010, the company was granted the *Navratna* status by the Government of India. In September 2011, the government announced plans to divest 10% of its stake in RINL via an initial public offering.

Operations

RINL operates a 7.3 million tonne per annum capacity steel plant in Visakhapatnam.[6] During the initial periods, the company suffered huge losses. Later the profits have gone up by 200% making it the only steel industry to achieve such a target. Its annual capacity is expected to reach almost 7.5 million tonnes by 2020. RINL plans to invest ₹ 60,000 crore (US$8.4 billion) to increase the capacity to 20 million tonnes by 2027.[7]

RINL has successfully commissioned its next phase despite some major setbacks with blasts in its new blast furnace. Another unit of RINL is coming in Uttar Pradesh. With an investment of 1688 Crores, RINL is establishing a plant for Rail wheels under make in India initiative. This plant will be equipped with ultra-modern technology. It will produce 1 lakh wheels per year.

REC Limited

Jump to navigationJump to search

This article **needs additional citations for verification**. Please help improve this article by adding citations to reliable sources. Unsourced material may be challenged and removed. *Find sources:* "REC Limited" – news · newspapers · books · scholar · JSTOR *(September 2019) (Learn how and when to remove this template message)*

REC Limited

आरईसी
REC
असीमित ऊर्जा, अनन्त संभावनाएं
Endless energy. Infinite possibilities.

REC corporate office on Lodhi Road, New Delhi.

Native name	आई ई सी लिमिटेड
Formerly	Rural Electrification Corporation Limited
Type	Public Sector Undertaking
Traded as	BSE: 532955 NSE: RECLTD
Industry	Infrastructure finance
Founded	25 July 1969; 51 years ago New Delhi, India
Headquarters	Core-4, SCOPE Complex, 7, Lodhi Road, New Delhi, India
Area served	India
Key people	Ajeet Kumar Agarwal (CMD)

Revenue	▲₹30,007.50 crore (US$4.2 billion) (2020)
Operating income	▲₹26,021.28 crore (US$3.6 billion) (2020)
Net income	▲₹4,972.27 crore (US$700 million) (2020)
Total assets	▲₹347,030.08 crore (US$49 billion) (2020)
Total equity	▲₹35,396.43 crore (US$5.0 billion) (2020)
Owner	Power Finance Corporation (52.63%)
Number of employees	487 (March 2019)
Subsidiaries	REC Transmission Projects Company Limited (RECTPCL) REC Power Distribution Company Limited (RECPDCL)
Website	www.recindia.nic.in

REC Limited, formerly **Rural Electrification Corporation Limited,** is a public Infrastructure Finance Company in India's power sector. The company is a Public Sector Undertaking and finances and promotes rural electrification projects across India. The company provides loans to Central/ State Sector Power Utilities in the country, State Electricity Boards, Rural Electric Cooperatives, NGOs and Private Power Developers.

On 7 December, 2018, the Cabinet Committee of Economic Affairs gave its in-principle approval for the sale of 52.63% REC to the state-owned Power Finance Corporation (PFC).[4] On 20 March 2019, PFC signed the agreement to acquire a 52.63% controlling stake in REC for ₹ 14,500 crore (US$2.0 billion). On 28 March, PFC announced that it had completed making the payment for the acquisition and intended to merge REC with itself in 2020.

Business operations

REC is a Navratna Company functioning under the purview of the Ministry of Power. The company is listed on both National Stock Exchange and Bombay Stock Exchange. Business operations in India are supported by a network of 13 Project Offices and 5 Zonal Offices, headquartered in New Delhi.

Services

The company is primarily engaged in providing finance for rural electrification projects across India and provides loans to Central/ State Sector Power Utilities, State Electricity Boards, Rural Electric Cooperatives, NGOs and Private Power Developers. The company sanctions loan as a sole lender or co-lender or in consortium with or without the status of lead financer. It also provides consultancy, project monitoring and financial/ technical appraisal support for projects, also in the role of nodal agency for Government of India schemes or projects. It engages in ascertaining financial requirements of power utilities in the country in the T&D sector along with appraising T&D schemes for financing. REC has financed T&D schemes for system improvement, intensive electrification, pump-set energisation and APDRP Programme. The company is also actively involved in physical as well as financial monitoring of T&D schemes.

REC also offers loan products for financing Renewable Energy projects. The company has tied up a line of credit for US$ 100 M (approximately ₹ 6000 M) with KfW under Indo-German Development Cooperation for financing renewable energy power projects at concessional rates of interest. Eligible projects include solar, wind, small hydro, biomass power, and cogeneration power and hybrid projects

GARV APP is an application developed and maintained by REC, incepted to aid the Grameen Vidyutikaran Mission running under DDUGJY (Deen Dayal Upadhyaya Gram Jyoti Yojana). The App "GARV" (Grameen Vidyutikaran), which provides real-time updates on electrification status of 18452 UE villages, was launched on 14th Oct, 2015. The Mobile app is accessible to all stakeholders including the general public at large.

Finances

The Company was listed on the National Stock Exchange and the Bombay Stock Exchange on 12 March 2008. REC went for Initial Public Offer of 156,120,000 Equity Shares in February 2008 which was oversubscribed by about 27 times, raising a total amount of ₹ 819 crores. Further Public Offer of 171,732,000 equity shares was made in February 2010. The issue was oversubscribed by 3.14 times, raising a total of ₹ 26.47 billion

The company is currently among the top 500 Global Financial Services brands by UK-based plc Brand Finance. The company is also among the Forbes Global 2000 companies for 2010. Domestic debt instruments of REC are assigned the highest rating "AAA" by credit rating agencies CRISIL, Fitch and ICRA. Moody's and Fitch have rated its international credit rating at par with India's sovereign rating.

International collaborations have included past tie-ups for External Commercial Borrowings with Standard Chartered Bank (London), DEPFA Investment Bank Limited (Cyprus) etc. as well as current tie-ups with KfW (Germany) and Japan International Cooperation Agency (Japan) under Official Development Assistance. As an IFC, REC can also issue Infrastructure Bonds and raise funds up to US$500 M through External Commercial Borrowing in a year.

IPO & FPO

History

Early years

REC was set up in July 1969, in the backdrop of a critical drought situation facing India in the late sixties. The company's initial mandate was mainly to help State Electricity Boards energise pump-sets across the country to boost agriculture and overcome the crippling impact of three successive years of deficient monsoons. The company also provided finance to accelerate the pace of rural electrification in the overall context of planned programmes for increased agricultural production. Besides finance, REC also offered appraising, consultancy, technical support and monitoring of projects, to assist State Electricity Boards/Power Utilities, Rural Electric Cooperatives and other such institutions.

Post-Liberalised India (1990s)

Liberalisation by the Government of India (GoI) in 1991 saw introduction of amendments to existing laws and reform measures enabling the private sector to participate in large-scale in manufacturing industry, services industry and infrastructure. Sectors like power, airports, seaports, roadways, projects were identified for private participation, and nodal agencies were set up to do the initial spade work and later hand over such projects to private players through competitive bidding routes. In April 2006, GOI identified 14 transmission projects worth ₹ 200 billion for development by 2012. REC was identified as one of the two GOI-appointed nodal agencies for transferring identified projects to private developers. REC also started extending loans to manufacturers of T&D equipment.

2000–Current

Till 2000, REC focused on the Transmission and Distribution aspect of power, with projects for household electrification in rural and semi-urban areas, area electrification in tribal/Dalit areas, intensive electrification, and system improvement projects based on strengthening and improving transmission, sub-transmission and distribution systems. REC's portfolio of Generation projects constituted mainly Mini/Micro Generation Projects up to 25 MW capacity till 2000. In June 2002, the mandate of REC was expanded to include financing of all generation projects without limit on size or location. Today, financing of Generation projects has become a major thrust-area of operations for REC, also attracting majority of its private sector borrowers.

Since 2005, REC has been appointed nodal agency by Ministry of Power [1] for Government of India scheme Rajiv Gandhi Grameen Vidyutikaran Yojana aimed at building rural electricity infrastructure and household electrification towards the National Common Minimum Programme goal of access to electricity for all. Under the scheme, 90% capital subsidy is provided by Government of India for overall cost of projects. Cumulatively till FY10, works in 190,858 villages have been completed and free connections to over 10 million below poverty line (BPL) households have been released. The REC is the nodal agency under the newly launched SAUBHAGYA Yojana by the present Modi government.

Philanthropic Activities

During Corona Pandemic, REC tied up with TAJSATS to provide nutritious food to 300 frontline workers daily. It has distributed

4.58 lakh kg of foodgrains, 1.26 lakh meal packets, 9,600 liters of sanitizers, 3,400 PPE kits and 83,000 masks to fight coronavirus pandemic.

REC Institute of Power Management and Training (RECIPMT)

In 1979, REC established a national training institute in Hyderabad for the development of techno-managerial skill and efficiency in State Electricity Boards (SEBs), Distribution Companies, Rural Electric Cooperatives and other Power Utilities, and also to conduct in-house training programmes for REC's employees. CIRE also served as a platform for association with other institutions towards a common goal of Rural Electrification (RE) and rural energy development.

Today, RECIPMT conducts regular programmes on various aspects of Transmission and Distribution for national and international executives in the power sector, including seminars participated by both private and public utilities. Programmes focus on adoption of innovative and cost effective modern technologies, training in both conventional and non-conventional energy areas and practical demonstrations via an in-house Energy Park.

Energy Efficiency Services Limited (EESL)

EESL is a joint venture (JV) with 4 power PSUs – REC, Power Grid, NTPC, and PFC for implementing energy efficiency projects, promoting usage of energy efficient appliances, promoting the concept of Energy Service Companies (ESCOs) etc.

Indian Energy Exchange (IEX)

REC is an equity partner in Indian Energy Exchange (IEX)[2], India's first nationwide, automated, and online electricity trading platform (power exchange/ electricity market), among other reputed investors like IDFC, Adani, Reliance Energy, Lanco and Tata Power.

Shipping Corporation of India

Trade name	BSE: 523598 NSE: SCI
Type	Public Sector Undertaking
Industry	Shipping
Founded	Mumbai, 2 October 1961
Headquarters	Mumbai
Key people	Mrs H.K Joshi (Chairman & MD)
Revenue	▲₹4,425.44 crore (US$620 million) (2020)
Operating income	▲₹711.64 crore (US$100 million) (2020)
Net income	▲₹302.35 crore (US$42 million) (2020)
Total assets	▼₹13,733.12 crore (US$1.9 billion) (2020)
Total equity	▲₹7,298.18 crore (US$1.0 billion) (2020)
Owner	Government of India (63.75%)
Number of employees	675 (July 2019)
Website	shipindia.com

The Shipping Corporation of India (SCI) is a Government of India Public Sector Enterprise with its headquarters in Mumbai, Maharashtra, India that operates and manages vessels that services both national and international lines.

History

SCI Head Office at Nariman Point Mumbai

SCI was established on 2 October 1961 by the amalgamation of Eastern Shipping Corporation and Western Shipping Corporation. Two more shipping companies, Jayanti Shipping Company and Mogul Lines Limited, were merged with SCI in 1973 and 1986 respectively.

SCI started out with 19 vessels. It gradually metamorphosed into a conglomerate having 80 ships of 59 lakh (5.9 million) tonnes deadweight (DWT) with interests in different segments of the shipping trade.

SCI was also awarded the prestigious "*Navratna*" status by the Indian Government in 2008.

On the 21st of November 2019, the Government of India approved the privatisation of SCI.

Chapter 5

Transport in India

Introduction

Transport and Communication are the most fundamental infrastructure of any economic development of any country. While manufacturing capital and consumers goods in the Indian factories, these goods need to be transported from factory place to the market place so that there will be sale of these goods to the public.

In order to move goods from one place to others as well as the employees from their residence to the office and visa-a-versa. It is necessary that transport system should be modernised and up-to-date.

There are mainly three types of transport systems. (1) Road, (2) Railways and (3) navigation by water.

These three ways of transport are developed in India. During the British rule, transport facilities were developed to promote their export trade in India such as railways, roads etc.

Goods are carried away by road via trucks. Large trucks accept goods and road receipt or lorry receipt are issued to the person who delivers the goods. These goods are loaded on the Lorry or Truck and sent to the destination where the buyer will take delivery of the goods. The Lorry receipt is sent to the buyer by the seller who takes delivery of the goods in exchange of Lorry receipt at the destination of the buyer when the lorry arrives on the destination.

In case of goods sent by the seller by railway wagons, the Rail Receipt is received which is sent to the buyer and buyer on showing and submitting this RR will receive goods at his destination for operations of the goods.

In case of navigation of water, very large size capital goods machinery are sent through Ships or vessels. Bill of Lading is issued to the seller on the port where goods are delivered at the departed port to deliver them to the buyer on designated port. Seller will send Bill of Lading to the buyer. On arrival of the Ship/vessels on designated port, the buyer will submit the B/L to the shipping agency and will clear his goods for further operations.

In case of air, small size goods are sent by the seller to the buyer and Air Receipt for receiving goods is issued by the Air Company to the seller. Seller will send the Air Receipt to buyer who will submit it to the Air Authorities to clear the goods by the buyer for further operations.

Transport of human beings from one place to other places is done by the railways, Lorries, buses, airplanes and ships in large number. This promotes trade and production and therefore market and economic conditions of any country tremendously.

India has large infrastructure facilities in constructing Highways, ports, improved road and providing improved navigation facilities to the Indian citizens. Air transport is also improved.

Allied industries developed with this are construction of ships, manufacturing passenger cars and goods wagons as well as building large airplanes and railway goods wagons and railway racks.

All these provide large employment to the Indian citizens.

Recently in Lockdown situation on account of Corona Virus, we have seen the importance of transportation. Transport was entirely locked down and our life became standstill. For improvement of the same, we are eagerly waiting for removing of lock down to improve our standard of lives.

Transport in India consists of transport by land, water and air. Public transport is the primary mode of road transport for most of the Indian citizens, and India's public transport systems are among the most heavily used in the world.

India's road network is the second-largest and one of the busiest in the world, transporting 8.225 billion passengers and over 980 million tonnes of cargo annually, as of 2015. India's rail network is the fourth largest and second busiest in the world, transporting 8.44 billion passengers and 1.23 billion tonnes of freight annually, as of 2019.

Aviation in India is broadly divided into military and civil aviation which is the fastest-growing aviation market in the world (IATA data) and Bangaluru with 65% national share is the largest aviation manufacturing hub of India. India's waterways network, in the form of rivers, canals, backwaters and creeks, is the ninth largest waterway network in the world. Freight transport by waterways is highly under-utilised in India with the total cargo moved (in ton kilometres) by inland waterways being 0.1 percent of the total inland traffic in India. Roads in India are maintained by National Highway Authority of India (NHAI).

In total, about 21 percent of households have two wheelers whereas 4.7 percent of households in India have cars or vans as per the 2011 Census. The automobile industry in India is currently rapidly growing with an annual production of over 4.6 million vehicles, with an annual growth rate of 10.5% and vehicle volume is expected to rise greatly in the future.

Human/Animal powered

Walking

Walking has constituted a major form of transport in ancient times. This mode of transport has always been a first foot for humans. People used to cover long distances on foot or bullock carts. For instance, Adi Sankaracharya travelled all over India from Kalady near Kochi. Walking still constitutes an important mode of transport in rural areas. In the city of Mumbai, to further improve the transit conditions for pedestrians, the Mumbai Metropolitan Region Development Authority, has commenced the construction of more than 50 skywalks, as part of the Mumbai Skywalk project, which is very helpful as walk enthusiasts take part in reducing traffic. The Dakshineswar skywalk has also come up in West Bengal.

Palanquins

A palanquin in Calcutta

Royal palanquin of Mehrangarh Fort

Palanquins are also known as *palkis*, was one of the luxurious methods primarily used by the rich and noblemen for travelling and also to carry a deity (idol) of a God. Many temples have sculptures of God being carried in *palkis*. Modern use of the palanquin is limited to Indian weddings, pilgrimage and carrying idols of Gods.

Bullock carts/Horse carriages

Bullock carts have been traditionally used for transport, especially in rural India. The arrival of the British saw drastic improvements in the horse carriages which were used for transport since early days. Today, they are used in smaller towns and are referred as Tanga or *buggies*. Victorias of Mumbai which were used for tourist purposes, are now banned and plans are afloat to replace it with Victoria styled electric carriages. Horse carriages are now rarely found in the cities of India barring tourist areas and hill stations. In recent years cities have banned the movement of slow moving vehicles on the main roads.

Bicycles

Bicycles or cycles, have ownership rates ranging from around 30% to 75% at the state level. Along with walking, cycling accounts for 50 to 80% of the commuter trips for those in the informal sector in urban areas. However, recent developments suggest that bicycle riding is quickly becoming popular in the metropolitan cities of India. Today, government development authorities all over India encourages the setup and use of separate bicycle lanes alongside the roads to combat pollution and ease traffic congestion.

Human-pulled rickshaws

Human-pulled rickshaws are nowadays rarely available in various cities and villages in the country. Many local governments have proposed a ban on these rickshaws describing them as "inhuman". But in reality the rickshaws are still not yet banned. The Government of West Bengal proposed a ban on these rickshaws in 2005. Though a bill aiming to address this issue, termed as Calcutta Hackney Carriage Bill, was passed by the West Bengal Assembly in 2006, it has not been implemented yet. The Government of West Bengal is working on an amendment to this bill to avoid the loopholes that got exposed when the Hand-pulled Rickshaw Owners' Association filed a petition against the bill.

Cycle rickshaws

Cycle rickshaw

Cycle rickshaws were introduced in India in the 1940s. They are bigger than a tricycle where two people sit on an elevated seat at the back and a person pedals from the front. In the late 2000s, they were banned in several cities for causing traffic congestion. The Delhi Police recently submitted an affidavit against plying of cycle rickshaws to ease traffic congestion in the city but it was dismissed by the Delhi High Court In addition, environmentalists have supported the retention of cycle rickshaws as a non-polluting mode of transport.[28]

Road

Main article: Roads in India

The Mumbai-Pune Expressway was the first expressway to be operational in India in 1995

Bandra-Worli Bridge in Mumbai

As per 2017 estimates, the total road length in India is 5,603,293 km (3,481,725 mi); making the Indian road network the second largest road network in the world after the United States. At 0.66 km of highway per square kilometer of land the density of India's highway network is higher than that of the United States (0.65) and far higher than that of China's (0.16) or Brazil's (0.20).

India has a network of National Highways connecting all the major cities and state capitals, forming the economic backbone of the country. As of 2013, India has a total of 70,934 km (44,076 mi) of National Highways, of which 1,205 km (749 mi) are classified as expressways. Although India has large network of four or more lane highways of international quality standards, but without access control (entry/exit control), they are not called as expressways but simply as highways.

As per the National Highways Authority of India, about 65% of freight and 80% passenger traffic is carried by the roads. The National Highways carry about 40% of total road traffic, though only about 2% of the road network is covered by these roads. Average growth of the number of vehicles has been around 10.16% per annum over recent years.

Under National Highways Development Project (NHDP), work is under progress to equip national highways with at least four lanes; also there is a plan to convert some stretches of these roads to six lanes. All national highways are metaled, but very few are constructed of concrete, the most notable being the Mumbai-Pune Expressway. In recent years construction has commenced on a nationwide system of multi-lane highways, including the Golden Quadrilateral and North-South and East-West Corridors which link the largest cities in India.

In 2000, around 40% of villages in India lacked access to all-weather roads and remained isolated during the monsoon season. To improve rural connectivity, *Pradhan Mantri Gram Sadak Yojana* (Prime Minister's Rural Road Program), a project funded by the Central Government with the help of World Bank, was launched in 2000 to build all-weather roads to connect all habitations with a population of 500 or above (250 or above for hilly areas).

Type of Road	***Length***
Expressways	1,206 km (749 mi) as of 2011
National Highways	79,116 km (49,160 mi)
State Highways	155,716 km (96,757 mi)
District and Rural Roads	4,455,010 km (2,768,210 mi)
Total Length	4,689,842 km (2,914,133 mi) (Approx)

Bus

Mumbai's B.E.S.T. is India's oldest operating transport body

Buses are an important means of public transport in India. Due to this social significance, urban bus transport is often owned and operated by public agencies, and most state governments operate bus services through a State Road Transport Corporation. These corporations have proven extremely useful in connecting villages and towns across the country. Alongside the public companies there are many private bus fleets: As of 2012, there were 131,800 publicly owned buses in India, but 1,544,700 buses owned by private companies.

However, the share of buses is negligible in most Indian cities as compared to personalised vehicles, and two-wheelers and cars account for more than 80 percent of the vehicle population in most large cities.[36]

Bus Rapid Transit System

Ahmedabad BRTS

A KSRTC Volvo Bus. Such buses are common across the country.

TATA Motors Plant in Pune, Maharashtra.

Bus rapid transit systems (BRTS), exist in several cities of the country. Buses take up over 90% of public transport in Indian cities, and serve as an important mode of transport. Services are mostly run by state government owned Transport Corporations. In 1990s all government State Transport Corporations have introduced various facilities like low-floor buses for the disabled and air-conditioned buses to attract private car owners to help decongest roads. The Ahmedabad Bus Rapid Transport System, in 2010 won the prestigious Sustainable Transport Award from the Transportation Research Board in Washington.

Rainbow BRTS in Pune is the first BRTS system in the country. Mumbai introduced air conditioned buses in 1998. Bangaluru was the first city in India to introduce Volvo B7RLE intra-city buses in India in January 2005.

Bangaluru is the first Indian city to have an air-conditioned bus stop, located near Cubbon Park. It was built by Airtel. The city of Chennai houses one of Asia's largest bus terminus, the Chennai Mofussil Bus Terminus.

Motor vehicles

Two-wheelers

Motorcycles parked in Ladakh.

Motorised two-wheeler vehicles like scooters motorcycles and mopeds are very popular mode of transport due to their fuel efficiency and ease of use in congested roads or streets. The number of two-wheelers sold is several times to that of cars. There were 47.5 million powered two-wheelers in India in 2003 compared with just 8.6 million cars.

Manufacture of motorcycles in India started when Royal Enfield began assembly in its plant in Chennai in 1948. Royal Enfield, an iconic brand name in the country, manufactures different variants of the British Bullet motorcycle which is a classic motorcycle that is still in production. Hero MotoCorp (formerly ro Honda), Honda, Bajaj Auto, Yamaha, TVS Motors and Mahindra 2 Wheelers are the largest two-wheeler companies in terms of market-share.

Manufacture of scooters in India started when *Automobile Products of India (API)*, set up at Mumbai and incorporated in 1949, began assembling Innocenti-built Lambretta scooters in India. They eventually acquired licence for the Li150 series model, of which they began full-fledged production from the early sixties onwards. In 1972, *Scooters India Ltd (SIL)*, a state-run enterprise based in Lucknow,

Uttar Pradesh, bought the entire manufacturing rights of the last Innocenti Lambretta model. API has infrastructural facilities at Mumbai, Aurangabad, and Chennai but has been non-operational since 2002. SIL stopped producing scooters in 1998.

Motorcycles and scooters can be rented in many cities, Wicked Ride, Metro bikes and many other companies are working with state governments to solve last mile connectivity problems with mass transit solutions. Wearing protective headgear is mandatory for both the rider and the pillion-rider in most cities.

Automobiles

Private automobiles account for 30% of the total transport demand in urban areas of India. An average of 963 new private vehicles are registered every day in Delhi alone. The number of automobiles produced in India rose from 6.3 million in 2002–03 to 11 million (11.2 million) in 2008–09. There is substantial variation among different cities and states in terms of dependence on private cars: Bangaluru, Chennai, Delhi and Kolkata have 185, 127, 157 and 140 cars per 1,000 people respectively. This reflects different levels of urban density and varied qualities of public transport infrastructure. Nationwide, India still has a very low rate of car ownership. When comparing car ownership between BRIC developing countries, it is on a par with China, and exceeded by Brazil and Russia.

Compact cars, especially hatchbacks predominate due to affordability, fuel efficiency, congestion, and lack of parking space in most cities. Chennai is known as the "Detroit of India" for its automobile industry. Maruti, Hyundai and Tata Motors are the most popular brands in the order of their market share. The Ambassador once had a monopoly but is now an icon of pre-liberalisation India, and is still used by taxi companies. Maruti 800 launched in 1984 created the first revolution in the Indian auto sector because of its low pricing. It had the highest market share until 2004, when it was overtaken by other low-cost models from Maruti such as the Alto and the Wagon R, the Indica from Tata Motors and the Santro from Hyundai. Over the 20-year period since its introduction, about 2.4 million units of the Maruti 800 have been sold. However, with the launch of the Tata Nano, the least expensive production car in the world, Maruti 800 lost its popularity.

India is also known for a variety of indigenous vehicles made in villages out of simple motors and vehicle spare-parts. A few of these innovations are the Jugaad, *Maruta, Chhakda, Peter Rehda* and the *Fame.*

In the city of Bangaluru, Radio One and the Bangaluru Traffic Police, launched a carpooling drive which has involved celebrities such as Robin Uthappa, and Rahul Dravid encouraging the public to carpool. The initiative got a good response, and by the end of May 2009, 10,000 people are said to have carpooled in the city.

There have been efforts to improve the energy efficiency of transport systems in Indian cities, including by introducing performance standards for private automobiles or by banning particularly polluting older cars. The city of Kolkata, for example, passed a law in 2009/10 phasing out vehicles over 15 years old with the purpose of reducing air pollution in the city. However, the distributional effects were mixed. On the one hand, poorer urban residents are more likely to see public health improvements from better air quality, since they are more likely to live in polluted areas and work outdoors than richer urban residents. On the other hand, drivers of such vehicles suffered from losing their livelihoods as a result of this environmental regulation.

Utility vehicles

The first utility vehicle in India was manufactured by Mahindra. It was a copy of the original Jeep and was manufactured under licence. The vehicle was an instant hit and made Mahindra one of the top companies in India. The Indian Army and police extensively use Mahindra vehicles along with Maruti Gypsys for transporting personnel and equipment.

Tata Motors, the automobile manufacturing arm of the Tata Group, launched its first utility vehicle, the Tata Sumo, in 1994. The Sumo, owing to its then-modern design, captured a 31% share of the market within two years. The Tempo Trax from Force Motors till recently was ruling the rural areas. Sports utility vehicles now form a sizeable part of the passenger vehicle market.[74] Models from Tata, Honda, Hyundai, Ford, Chevrolet and other brands are available.

Taxis

Ambassador taxi in Kolkata

Most of the taxicabs in Kolkata and Mumbai are either Premier Padmini or Hindustan Ambassador cars. In rest of cities all modern cars are available. However, foreign developed app based taxi services like Uber as well as an Indian developed app based taxi services like Ola coming to the fore, taxicabs now include Sedans SUVs and even motorcycle taxis. Depending on the city/state, taxis can either be hailed or hired from taxi-stands. In cities such as Bangalore, Chennai, Hyderabad and Ahmedabad, taxis need to be hired over phone, whereas in cities like Kolkata and Mumbai, taxis can be hailed on the street. According to Government of India regulations, all taxis are required to have a fare-meter installed. There are additional surcharges for luggage, late-night rides and toll taxes are to be paid by the passenger. Since 2006, radio taxis have become increasingly popular with the public due to reasons of safety and convenience.

In cities and localities where taxis are expensive or do not charge as per the government or municipal regulated fares, people use share taxis. These are normal taxis which carry one or more passengers travelling to destinations either on one route to the final destination, or near the final destination. The passengers are charged according to the number of people with different destinations. The city of Mumbai will soon be the first city in India, to have an "in-taxi" magazine, titled *MumBaee*, which will be issued to taxis which are part of the Mumbai Taxi men's Union. The magazine debuted on 13 July 2009. In Kolkata, there are many *no refusal taxi* available with white and blue in colour.

Auto

An LPG Autorikshaw in Green, Delhi, India.

An auto is a three-wheeler vehicle for hire that does not have doors and is generally characterised by a small cabin for the driver in the front and a seat for passengers in the rear. Generally it is painted in yellow, green or black colour and has a black, yellow or green canopy on the top, but designs vary considerably from place to place. The colour of the auto-rickshaw is also determined by the fuel that it is powered by, for example, Agartala, Ahmedabad, Mumbai, Pune and Delhi have green or black autos indicating the use of compressed natural gas(CNG), whereas the autos of Kolkata, Bangaluru, Hyderabad have green autos indicating the use of LPG.

In Mumbai and other metropolitan cities, 'autos' or 'rickshaws', as they are popularly known, have regulated metered fares. A recent law prohibits auto rickshaw drivers from charging more than the specified fare, or charging night-fare before midnight, and also prohibits the driver from refusing to go to a particular location. Mumbai and Kolkata are also the only two cities which prohibit auto rickshaws from entering a certain part of the city, in these cases being South Mumbai and certain parts of Downtown Kolkata. However, in cities like Chennai, it is common to see autorickshaw drivers demand more than the specified fare and refuse to use fare meter.

Airports and railway stations at many cities such as Howrah, Chennai and Bangaluru provide a facility of prepaid auto booths, where the passenger pays a fixed fare as set by the authorities for various locations.

Electric rickshaw is new popular means of transport, rapidly growing in number in India, due to low running and initial cost, other economic and environmental benefits, these vehicles are becoming popular in India. E-Rickshaws are made in fiberglass or metal body, powered by a BLDC Electric Motor with max power 2000 W and speed 25 km/h.

Rail

Main articles: Rail transport in India and Indian Railways

Chhatrapati Shivaji Maharaj railway station entrance

The dining saloon of the luxurious Maharajas' Express.

Country-wide rail services in India, are provided by the state-run Indian Railways under the supervision of the Ministry of Railways. IR is divided into eighteen zones including the Kolkata Metro Railway. The IR are further sub-divided into sixty seven divisions, each having a divisional headquarters.

The railway network travels across the country, covering more than 7,321 stations over a total route length of more than 67,415 km (41,890 mi) and track length of about 123,542 km (76,765 mi) as of March 2019. About 34,319 km (21,325 mi) or 50.90% of the route-kilometer was electrified as on March 2019. IR provides an important mode of transport in India, transporting 23.1 million passengers and 3.3 million tons of freight daily as on March 2019. IR is the world's eighth-largest employer, it had 1.227 million employees as of March 2019. As to rolling stock, IR owns over 289,185 (freight) wagons, 74,003 coaches and 12,147 locomotives as of March 2019. It also owns locomotive and coach production facilities. It operates both long distance and suburban rail systems.

The IR runs a number of special types of services which are given higher priority. The fastest train at present is the Vande Bharat Express with operation speeds of up to 180 km/h, though the fastest service is Gatimaan Express with an operational speed of 160 km/h (99 mph) and average speed of 100 km/h (62 mph), since the Vande Bharat Express is capped at 120 km/h for safety reasons. The Rajdhani trains introduced in 1969 provides connectivity between the national capital, Delhi and capitals of the states. On the other hand, Shatabdi Express provides connectivity between centres of tourism, pilgrimage or business. The Shatabdi Express trains run over short to medium distances and do not have sleepers while the Rajdhani Express runs over longer distances and have only sleeping accommodation. Both series of trains have a maximum permissible speed of 110 to 140 km/h (81 to 87 mph) but average speed of less than 100 km/h.

Besides, the IR also operates a number of luxury trains which cater to various tourist circuits. For instance, the Palace on Wheels serves the Rajasthan circuit and The Golden Chariot serves the Karnataka and Goa circuits. There are two UNESCO World Heritage Sites on IR, the Chhatrapati Shivaji Maharaj Terminus and the Mountain railways of India. The latter consists of three separate railway lines located in different parts of India, the Darjeeling Himalayan Railway, a 610 mm (2 ft) narrow gauge railway in Lesser Himalayas in West Bengal, the Nilgiri Mountain Railway, a 1,000 mm (3 ft 3 3/8 in) metre gauge rack railway in the Nilgiri Hills in Tamil Nadu and the Kalka-Shimla Railway, a 762 mm (2 ft 6 in) narrow gauge railway in the Siwalik Hills in Himachal Pradesh.

In the freight segment, IR ferries various commodities and fuels in industrial, consumer, and agricultural segments across the length and breadth of India. IR has historically subsidised the passenger segment with income from the freight business. As a result, freight services are unable to compete with other modes of transport on both cost and speed of delivery, leading to continuous erosion of market share. To counter this downward trend, IR has started new initiatives in freight segments including upgrading of existing goods sheds, attracting private capital to build multi-commodity multi-modal logistics terminals, changing container sizes, operating time-tabled freight train, and tweaking with the freight pricing/product mix.

In 1999, the Konkan Railway Corporation introduced the Roll on Roll off (RORO) service, a unique road-rail synergy system, on the section between Kolad in Maharashtra and Verna in Goa, which was extended up to Surathkal in Karnataka in 2004. The RORO service, the first of its kind in India, allowed trucks to be transported on flatbed trailers. It was highly popular, carrying about 110,000 trucks and bringing in about ₹ 740 million worth of earnings to the corporation till 2007.

Perhaps the game-changer for IR in the freight segment are the new dedicated freight corridors that are expected to be completed by 2020. When fully implemented, the new corridors, spanning around 3300 km, could support hauling of trains up to 1.5 km in length with 32.5-ton axle-load at speeds of 100 kilometres per hour (62 mph). Also, they will free-up capacity on dense passenger routes and will allow IR to run more trains at higher speeds. Additional corridors are being planned to augment the freight infrastructure in the country.

Commuter rail transport

In many Indian metropolitan regions, rail is the more efficient and affordable mode of public transport for daily commute. Examples of types of services include long-established local or suburban rail services such as Mumbai, the century-old tram service in Kolkata, the more recent metro service in Delhi, and Monorail feeder service in Mumbai.

Suburban rail

Mumbai suburban rail station.

Main article: Urban rail transit in India

The Mumbai Suburban Railway is the first rail system in India which began services in Mumbai in 1853, transports 6.3 million passengers daily and has the highest passenger density in the world. The Kolkata Suburban Railway, was established in Kolkata in 1854.

The operational suburban rail systems in India are in Mumbai Suburban Railway, Kolkata Suburban Railway, Lucknow-Kanpur Suburban Railway, Chennai Suburban Railway, Delhi Suburban Railway, Pune Suburban Railway, Hyderabad Multi-Modal Transport System, Barabanki-Lucknow Suburban Railway and Karwar railway division.

Other planned systems are Bengaluru Commuter Rail, Ahmedabad Suburban Railway and Coimbatore Suburban Railway.

Metro

Kochi Metro train at Palarivattom, Kerala.

Main article: Urban rail transit in India

The first modern rapid transit in India is the Kolkata Metro which started its operations in 1984 as the 17th Zone of the Indian Railways. The Delhi Metro in New Delhi is India's second conventional metro and began operations in 2002. The Namma Metro in Bangaluru is India's third operational rapid transit and began operations in 2011.

The operational systems are Kolkata Metro, Delhi Metro, Namma Metro, Rapid Metro, Mumbai Metro, Jaipur Metro, Chennai Metro, Kochi Metro, Lucknow Metro, Nagpur Metro and Hyderabad Metro.

The planned systems are Noida Metro, Ghaziabad Metro, Navi Mumbai Metro, Nagpur Metro, Metro-Link Express for Gandhinagar and Ahmedabad, Varanasi Metro, Kanpur Metro, Bareilly Metro, Pune Metro, Vijayawada Metro, Patna Metro, Meerut Metro, Guwahati Metro, Chandigarh Metro, Bhopal Metro, Kozhikode Light Metro, Indore Metro, Thiruvananthapuram Light Metro, Agra Metro, Coimbatore Metro, Visakhapatnam Metro, Surat Metro, Srinagar Metro, Greater Gwalior Metro, Jabalpur Metro, Greater Nashik Metro and Bengaluru Metro.

Currently, rapid transit is under construction or in planning in several major cities of India and will be opened shortly.

Monorail

A monorail in Mumbai

Monorail is generally considered as feeder system for the metro trains in India. In 2004, monorail was first proposed for Kolkata. But, later the idea was put on hold due to lack of funds and infeasibility.

The Mumbai Monorail, which started in 2014, is the first operational monorail network in India (excluding the Skybus Metro) since the Patiala State Monorail Trainways closed in 1927.

Other planned systems are Chennai Monorail, Kolkata Monorail, Allahabad Monorail, Bengaluru Monorail, Delhi Monorail, Indore Monorail, Kanpur Monorail, Navi Mumbai Monorail, Patna Monorail, Pune Monorail, Ahmedabad Monorail, Aizawl Monorail, Bhubaneswar Monorail, Jodhpur Monorail, Kota Monorail, Nagpur Monorail and Nashik Monorail.

Tram

Trams in Kolkata during the British colonial period.

In addition to trains, trams were introduced in many cities in late 19th century, though almost all of these were phased out. The trams in Kolkata is currently the only tram system in the country. The Calcutta Tramways Company is in the process of upgrading the existing tramway network at a cost of ₹ 240 million (US$3.4 million).

Metrolite

International links

Rail links between India and neighbouring countries are not well-developed. Two trains operate to Pakistan—the *Samjhauta Express* between Delhi and Lahore, and the *Thar Express* between Jodhpur and Karachi. Bangladesh is connected by a biweekly train, the *Maitree*

Express that runs from Kolkata to Dhaka and a weekly train, the *Bandhan Express* that runs from Kolkata to Khulna. Two rail links to Nepal exist—passenger services between Jainagar and Bijalpura, and freight services between Raxaul and Birganj.

No rail link exists with Myanmar but a railway line is to be built through from Jiribam (in Manipur) to Tamu through Imphal and Moreh. The construction of this missing link, as per the feasibility study conducted by the Ministry of External Affairs through RITES Ltd, is estimated to cost ₹ 29.41 billion (US$410 million). An 18 km railway link with Bhutan is being constructed from Hashimara in West Bengal to Toribari in Bhutan. No rail link exists with either China or Sri Lanka.

High-speed rail

India does not have any railways classified as high-speed rail (HSR), which have operational speeds in excess of 200 km/h (120 mph).

Prior to the 2014 general election, the two major national parties (Bharatiya Janata Party and Indian National Congress) pledged to introduce high-speed rail. The INC pledged to connect all of India's million-plus cities by high-speed rail, whereas BJP, which won the election, promised to build the Diamond Quadrilateral project, which would connect the cities of Chennai, Delhi, Kolkata, and Mumbai via high-speed rail. This project was approved as a priority for the new government in the incoming prime minister's speech. Construction of one kilometer of high speed railway track will cost ₹ 1 billion (US$14 million) – ₹ 1.4 billion (US$20 million) which is 10–14 times higher than the construction of standard railway. Indian government approved the choice of Japan to build India's first high-speed railway. The planned rail would run some 500 km (310 mi) between Mumbai and the western city of Ahmedabad, at a top speed of 320 km/h (200 mph). Under the proposal, construction is expected to begin in 2017 and be completed in 2023. It would cost about ₹ 980 billion (US$14 billion) and be financed by a low-interest loan from Japan. India will use the wheel-based 300 km/hr HSR technology, instead of new maglev 600 km/hr technology of the Japan used in Chuo Shinkansen. India is expected to have its HSR line operational from 2025 onwards, once the safety checks are completed.

Light rail

Like monorail, light rail is also considered as a feeder system for the metro systems. The planned systems are Kolkata Light Rail Transit and Delhi Light Rail Transit.

Airways

Air India, the flag carrier of India

Directorate General of Civil Aviation is the national regulatory body for the aviation industry. It is controlled by the Ministry of Civil Aviation. The ministry also controls aviation related autonomous organisations like the Airports Authority of India (AAI), Bureau of Civil Aviation Security (BCAS), Indira Gandhi Rashtriya Uran Akademi and Public Sector Undertakings including Air India, Pawan Hans Helicopters Limited and Hindustan Aeronautics Limited.

Air India is India's national flag carrier after merging with Indian (airline) in 2011 and plays a major role in connecting India with the rest of the world. IndiGo, Air India, Spicejet and GoAir are the major carriers in order of their market share. These airlines connect more than 80 cities across India and also operate overseas routes after the liberalisation of Indian aviation. Several other foreign airlines connect Indian cities with other major cities across the globe. However, a large section of country's air transport potential remains untapped, even though the Mumbai-Delhi air corridor was ranked the world's tenth busiest route by Amadeus in 2012.

Airports

Mumbai Airport Terminal

Prime Minister Narendra Modi at the inauguration of Paykong Airport, Sikkim.

While there are 346 civilian airfields in India – 253 with paved runways and 93 with unpaved runways, only 132 were classified as "airports" as of November 2014. Of these, Indira Gandhi International Airport in Delhi is the busiest in the country. The operations of the major airports in India have been privatised over the past five years and this has resulted in better equipped and cleaner airports. The terminals have either been refurbished or expanded.

India also has 33 "ghost airports," which were built in an effort to make air travel more accessible for those in remote regions but are now non-operational due to a lack of demand. The Jaisalmer Airport in Rajasthan, for example, was completed in 2013 and was expected to host 300,000 passengers a year but has yet to see any commercial flights take off. Despite the number of non-operational airports, India is currently planning on constructing another 200 "low-cost" airports over the next 20 years.

Length of runways	*Airports with paved runways*	*Airports with unpaved runways*
3,047 m (10,000 ft) or more	21	1
2,438 to 3,047 m (8,000 to 10,000 ft)	59	3
1,524 to 2,438 m (5,000 to 8,000 ft)	76	6
914 to 1,524 m (3,000 to 5,000 ft)	82	38
Under 914 m (3,000 ft)	14	45
Total	253	93

Heliports

Pawan Hans VT-PHA Helicopter.

As of 2013, there are 45 heliports in India. India also has the world's highest helipad at the Siachen Glacier at a height of 6400 m (21,000 ft) above mean sea level.

Pawan Hans Helicopters Limited is a public sector company that provides helicopter services to ONGC to its off-shore locations, and also to various State Governments in India, particularly in North-east India.

Water

India also has an extensive network of inland waterways.

Ports and shipping

Jawaharlal Nehru Port Trust in Navi Mumbai ranks 25th in the world as per container traffic.

International Container Transshipment Terminal at Kochi Port, the only transshipment facility in India. This port lies closest to international shipping routes among all Indian ports.

In India about 96% of the foreign trade by quantity and 70% by value takes place through the ports. Mumbai Port & JNPT(Navi Mumbai) handles 70% of maritime trade in India. There are twelve major ports: Navi Mumbai, Mumbai, Kochi, Kolkata (including Haldia), Paradip, Visakhapatnam, Ennore, Chennai, Thoothukudi, New Mangaluru, Mormugao and Kandla. Other than these, there are 187 minor and intermediate ports, 43 of which handle cargo.

Maritime transportation in India is managed by the Shipping Corporation of India, a government-owned company that also manages offshore and other marine transport infrastructure in the country. It owns and operates about 35% of Indian tonnage and operates in practically all areas of shipping business servicing both national and international trades. The only Indian state with three ports is Tamil Nadu, they are Ennore, Chennai and Tuticorin.

It has a fleet of 79 ships of 2,750,000 GT (4.8 million DWT) and also manages 53 research, survey and support vessels of 120,000 GT (060,000 DWT) on behalf of various government departments and other organisations. Personnel are trained at the Maritime Training Institute in Mumbai, a branch of the World Maritime University, which was set up in 1987. The Corporation also operates in Malta and Iran through joint ventures.

The distinction between major and minor ports is not based on the amount of cargo handled. The major ports are managed by port trusts which are regulated by the central government. They come under the purview of the Major Port Trusts Act, 1963. The minor ports are regulated by the respective state governments and many of these ports are private ports or captive ports. The total amount of traffic handled at the major ports in 2005–2006 was 382.33 Mt.

Inland Waterways

Main article: Inland Waterways Authority of India

A parked vessel along the Chapora River in Goa.

Boats sailing on National Waterway 2 at Guwahati

India has an extensive network of inland waterways in the form of rivers, canals, backwaters and creeks. The total navigable length is 14,500 kilometres (9,000 mi), out of which about 5,200 km (3,231 mi) of river and 485 km (301 mi) of canals can be used by mechanised crafts. Freight transport by waterways is highly underutilised in India compared to other large countries. The total cargo moved by inland waterways is just 0.15% of the total inland traffic in India, compared to the corresponding figures of 20% for Germany and 32% for Bangladesh.

Cargo that is transported in an organised manner is confined to a few waterways in Goa, West Bengal, Assam and Kerala. The Inland Waterways Authority of India (IWAI) is the statutory authority in charge of the waterways in India. It does the function of building the necessary infrastructure in these waterways, surveying the economic feasibility of new projects and also administration and regulation. The following waterways have been declared as National Waterways:

- **National Waterway 1:** Allahabad–Haldia stretch of the Ganga – Bhagirathi – Hooghly River system with a total length of 1,620 kilometres (1,010 mi) in 27 October 1986.
- **National Waterway 2:** *Saidiya*–Dhubri stretch of the Brahmaputra river system with a total length of 891 kilometres (554 mi) in 26 Oct 1988.
- **National Waterway 3:** Kollam–Kottapuram stretch of the West Coast Canal along with Champakara and Udyogmandal canals, with a total length of 205 kilometres (127 mi) in 1 Feb 1991.
- **National Waterway 4:** Bhadrachalam–Rajahmundry and Wazirabad–Vijaywada stretch of the Krishna–Godavari river system along with the Kakinada–Puduchery canal network, with a total length of 1,095 km (680 mi) in 24 Nov 2008.
- **National Waterway 5:** *Mangalgadi*–Paradeep and Talcher–*Dhamara* stretch of the Mahanadi–Brahmani river system along with the East Coast Canal, with a total length of 623 km (387 mi) in 24 Nov 2008.

Pipelines

Oil and gas industry in India imports 82% of its oil needs and aims to bring that down to 67% by 2022 by replacing it with local exploration, renewable energy and indigenous ethanol fuel (c. Jan 2018).

- Length of pipelines for crude oil is 20,000 km (12,427 mi).
- Length of Petroleum products pipeline is 15,000 kilometres (9,300 mi).

Logistics

Logistics in India ranking moved up to 35th place in 2016 from 54th in 2014 on World Bank's Global Logistics Performance Index. Government strategy aims to raise the share of global trade in India's GDP (US$2.7 trillion in FY 2017–18) to 40%, including half of it (20% of GDP) from exports (c. Jan 2018). Cost of logistics in India is 14% of GDP, which is higher than the developed nations, and government reforms aim to bring it down to 10% of GDP by 2022 (c. Jan 2018). Ministry of Commerce and Industry has created a new dedicated centralised Logistics division in collaboration with Singapore and Japan to handle the logistics which was earlier handled by several different ministries, such as railways, roads, shipping and aviation. To boot exports, each state will have exports and logistic policy and Nodal officers will be appointed at district level (c. Jan 2018). There are 64 transactions and 37 government agencies in the end-to-end production-to-export process. To further improve the ranking, improve speed of logistics, ease of doing business and reduce the cost of logistics, India is creating a *"common online integrated logistics e-marketplace portal"* that will cover all transactions in production and export, connect buyers with logistics service providers and government agencies such as the customs department Ice-gate system, Port Community Systems, Sea and Air Port terminals, Shipping lines, Railways, etc. (c. Jan 2018).

As part of the US$125 billion port-led development project Sagar-mala, government will define the regulatory framework for the Indian logistics operational standards by benchmarking India's 300 dry ports logistics parks (inland container depots or ICDs) to the top 10 logistics international best practices nations to boost exports, remove supply chain bottle necks, reduce transaction costs, optimize logistics mix, set up new hub-and-spoke dry ports (c. Jan 2018). To reduce the logistics costs by 10% and $C0_2$ emissions by 12%, the government is also developing 35 new *"Multimodal Logistics Parks"* (MMLPs) on 36 ring roads, which will facilitate 50% of the freight moved in India. Land has been earmarked and pre-feasibility study is underway for 6 of these MMLPs (c. May 2017).

Confederation of Indian Industry (CII) and government will organise an annual National Logistics convention. Major supply chain solution providers include Container Corporation of India and Transport Corporation of India, and magazine Logistics Management India magazine is one of the industry publication.

Modernisation

In 1998, the Supreme Court of India published a Directive that specified the date of April 2001 as deadline to replace or convert all buses, three-wheelers and taxis in Delhi to compressed natural gas.

The Karnataka State Road Transport Corporation was the first State Transport Undertaking in India to utilise bio-fuels and zethanol-blended fuels. KSRTC took an initiative to do research in alternative fuel forms by experimenting with various alternatives— blending diesel with biofuels such as honge, palm, sunflower, groundnut, coconut and sesame. In 2009, the corporation decided to promote the use of biofuel buses.

In 2017, the government announced that by 2030, only electric vehicles would be sold in the country. It also announced that by 2022 all trains would be electric trains.

Infrastructure Policy & Finance Division

MAJOR FUNCTIONS:

1. Matters relating to the Harmonised List of Infrastructure Sub-sectors.
2. All policy related issues in infrastructure sectors including those concerning road, ports, shipping, railways, inland water transport, urban development, power, new and renewable energy, railways and telecommunication sector referred to Department of Economic Affairs by the Administrative Ministries concerned.
3. Examination of proposals requiring the approval of EFC/PIB/CCEA/COS/CCI in above sectors for viability and justification. In addition, all matters relating to Delhi Mumbai Industrial Corridor Trust and DMICDC.
4. Matters relating to infrastructure financing and promotion of investments in infrastructure sectors and credit enhancement.

5. All International interface on infrastructure policy issues and infrastructure financing.
6. Matters relating to the Infrastructure and Investment Working Group (IIWG) of G-20.
7. All policy related issues pertaining to energy sector, viz., Petroleum & Natural Gas, Coal, Atomic Energy and New & Renewable Energy.
8. Examination of proposals for grant of viability gap funding (VGF) under the National Clean Energy Fund (NCEF); matters relating to OPEC Fund for International Development (OFID) and Committee on Allocation of Natural Resources (CANR).
9. Policy matters related to Public Private Partnerships (PPPs). The Public Private Partnership (PPP) Cell is responsible for matters concerning Public Private Partnerships, including policy, schemes and programmes and all other matters relating to mainstreaming PPPs.
10. Matters and proposals relating to the scheme for Financial support to Public Private Partnerships in Infrastructure [Viability Gap Funding (VGF)] Scheme and the India Infrastructure Project Development Fund.

SUBJECT/ SECTION- WISE ALLOCATION OF WORK

- Infrastructure - It consists of four sections which are:
  - Infrastructure (Policy) Cell
  - Infrastructure Financing
  - PPP Cell (Public Private partnership)
  - Energy Cell

NAME & CONTACT ADDRESS OF DIVISION HEAD

Dr Kumar Vinay Pratap

Joint Secretary (IPF),

Department of Economic Affairs,

Room No. 34-C,North Block,

New Delhi 110001.

Email: kv [dot] pratap [at] nic [dot] in

INFRASTRUCTURE & ENERGY DIVISION

(a) Infrastructure (Policy) Cell

- All policy related issues in infrastructure sector including those concerning roads, ports, shipping, railways, inland water transport, urban development, power and telecommunication sector referred to the Department of Economic Affairs (DEA) by the concerned administrative Ministries or identified and examined by DEA.
- Examination of proposals in above sectors requiring the approval of EFC/PIB/CCEA/COS/CCI for their viability and justification.
- Sectoral Charge – Ministry of Road Transport & Highways, Ministry of Shipping including Ports and Inland Water Transport, Ministry of Urban Development, Ministry of Railways, Ministry of Civil Aviation, Department of Telecommunication, Department of Post.
- All matters relating to Roads projects (PPP and non-PPP) including EFC/SFC/PPPAC and EI/EC under the Government of India VGF Scheme.
- Matters relating to Delhi Mumbai Industrial Corridor Trust and DMICDC.
- Development of Smart Cities.
- Atal Mission for Rejuvenation & Urban Transformation (AMRUT).
- Institutional Mechanism (IM) for Harmonised Master List of Infrastructure Sub-sectors.
- Telecom Commission
- National Highway Authority of India
- External charge – China, South Korea and North Korea
- India Korea Macro-economic and Financial Dialogue; and
- India – China Financial Dialogue.

Name and Designation of officers:

SECTION OFFICER	ASSISTANT DIRECTOR	DIRECTOR
	Tel: 23095158 I/Com : 5158 Room No. 242-C North Block	Tel: 2309 2528 I/Com: 5075 Room no: 61 North Block

(b) Infrastructure Finance Section

Functions:

- Matters related to infrastructure financing and promotion of investments in infrastructure sectors.
- Matters relating to Infrastructure Debt Funds (IDFs), Real Estate Investment Trusts (REITs)/Infrastructure Investment Trust InvITs, Tax Free Bonds, Municipal Bonds and other instruments meant for infrastructure financing and credit enhancements.
- All international interfaces on infrastructure financing (other than PPPs).
- Model Tripartite Agreements (MTA) for sectors such as Road, Ports, etc.
- External charge- Bahrain, Oman, Saudi Arabia, Qatar, Kuwait, UAE, Yemen, Israel, Jordan and Lebanon.
- Matters relating to Infrastructure and Investment Working Group (IIWG) of G-20.
- India-Saudi Joint Investment Fund, Indo-Israeli R & D Fund.
- Examination of proposals in above sectors requiring the approval of EFC/PIB/CCEA/COS/CCI for their viability and justification.
- All policy matters relating to Project Monitoring Group (PMG).
- India Saudi Arabia Joint Commission for Technical and Economic Cooperation.
- Matters relating to meetings of Board of Directors of ONGC-Videsh Limited (OVL), IIFCL and IRFC as Government nominee on the Board of Directors.
- Coordination and general matters pertaining to the Division.

Name and Designation of Officers:

SECTION OFFICER	ASSISTANT DIRECTOR	ADVISER
Tel : 2309 5162	Tel: 23093121	Telefax: 23092528
Intercom : 5162	I/Com: 5022	Intercom: 5075
Fax: 23093156	Fax: 23093156	
Room No: 273	Room No: 273	Room No: 61
North Block	North Block	North Block

(c) PUBLIC PRIVATE PARTNERSHIP (PPP) Cell

Policy matters related to Public Private Partnerships. The Public Private Partnership (PPP) Cell is responsible for matters concerning Public Private Partnerships, including policy, schemes, programmes and capacity building and all other matters relating to mainstreaming PPPs.

Functions:

1. Matters relating to appraisal and approval of Central sector PPP projects, as per the Cabinet approved "Compendium of Guidelines for Central Sector PPPs" and the Delegation of Powers assigned from time to time except those in Road Sector.
2. Matters and proposals relating to clearance by Public Private Partnership Appraisal Committee (PPPAC) accept those in Road Sector.
3. Matters and proposals relating to the scheme for Financial support to Public Private Partnerships in Infrastructure Viability Gap Funding (VGF) Scheme except those in Road Sector.
4. Matters and proposals relating to the scheme for India Infrastructure Project Development Fund (IIPDF).
5. Developing Multi-pronged and innovative interventions and support mechanisms for facilitating PPPs in the country, including Technical Assistance and programmes from bilateral/ multilateral agencies on mainstreaming PPPs and support to State and local governments.
6. Managing training programmes, strategies, exposures for capacity building for PPPs and other matters relating to institution building for mainstreaming PPPs.
7. All International interfaces on PPPs and other matters concerning PPPs.
8. Matters relating to management of PPP related information, including www.pppinindia.gov.in and infrastructureindia.gov.in.

Name and Designation of Officers:

SECTION OFFICER	DEPUTY DIRECTOR	DIRECTOR
Tel : 2309 5150	Tel: 23093404	
Intercom: 5150	Intercom: 5232	
Room No:251-C	Room No: 251-C	
North Block	North Block	-

(d) ENERGY CELL

Functions:

1. All policy related issues pertaining to energy sector viz. Petroleum and Natural Gas, Coal, Atomic Energy and New & Renewable Energy.
2. Sectoral Charge of M/o Petroleum and Natural Gas, M/o New and Renewable Energy, M/o Coal, Dept. of Atomic Energy and Dept. of Space.
3. Examination of the investment proposals in energy sector requiring the approval of Cabinet/CCI/CCEA/CoS/PIB/EFC for their viability and justification.
4. All matters relating to Power Sector (including Policy, Projects, DCNs/CCEA Notes/EFC/SFC, etc.).
5. Internal territorial charge of Chhattisgarh, Maharashtra, Gujarat and Madhya Pradesh.
6. External territorial charge of Iran, Iraq, Cyprus.
7. Examination of proposals for grant of viability gap funding under the National Clean Energy Fund (NCEF).
8. Matters relating to OPEC Fund for International Development (OFID).
9. Related to Committee on Allocation of Natural Resources (CANR).

Chapter 6

Defence Planning Committee

From Wikipedia, the free encyclopedia

Jump to navigationJump to search

Defence Planning Committee	
Committee overview	
Formed	19 April 2018; 2 years ago
Jurisdiction	India
Minister responsible	Rajnath Singh, Minister of Defence
Deputy Minister responsible	Shripad Yesso Naik, Minister of State for Defence
Committee executive	Ajit Doval, IPS, National Security Adviser and *ex-officio* chairperson
Parent department	Ministry of Defence, Government of India

The **Defence Planning Committee** is a senior decision-making organisation created on 19 April 2018 by the Government of India to facilitate comprehensive planning for the defence forces besides focusing on military doctrines to deal with emerging security challenges for India.

History

The Defence Planning Committee was notified by the Ministry of Defence (MoD) in April 2018, the National Security Adviser (NSA) was appointed as the chairperson of the committee, with the chairperson,

Chiefs of Staff Committee, three service chiefs (Chief of the Army Staff, Chief of the Air Staff and Chief of the Naval Staff), defence, foreign and expenditure secretaries being its members and the chief of the Integrated Defence Staff (CIDS) being its member-secretary, the NSA was also given the mandate to co-opt members as they see fit. The Integrated Defence Staff headquarters at Kashmir House, New Delhi was to serve as the committee's secretariat.

NSA Ajit Doval chaired the committee's first meeting on 3 May 2018, which was attended by the three chiefs of staff, and defence, foreign and expenditure secretaries. The first meeting discussed the topics under mandate of DC and ways to expedite modernisation of the armed forces and evolving a security strategy.

Mandate

The mandate of DPC is manifold; the committee is empowered to "analyze and evaluate all relevant inputs relating to defence planning", which consists of—amongst others—"national defence and security priorities, foreign policy imperatives, operational directives and associated requirements, relevant strategic and security-related doctrines, defence acquisition and infrastructure development plans, including the 15-year Long-Term Integrated Perspective Plan (LTIPP), defence technology and development of the Indian defence industry and global technological advancement".

The committee is also vested with the power of preparing different drafts, including—but not limited to—drafts on: "national security strategy, strategic defence review and doctrines; international defence engagement strategy; roadmap to build defence manufacturing eco-system; strategy to boost defence exports; and prioritised capability development plans for the armed forces over different time-frames in consonance with the overall priorities, strategies and likely resource flows.

The DPC answers to—and submits its reports to—the *Raksha Mantri* (Minister of Defence), currently Rajnath Singh.

According to the notification issued by Indian Government the DPC will have several mandates namely to:

1. Prepare a draft National Security Strategy.
2. Develop a capability development plan.

3. Work on defence diplomacy issues.
4. Improving defence manufacturing ecosystem in India.

DPC would also analyses all inputs relating to the defence planning and foreign policy imperatives. The committee would focus on the defence acquisition and infrastructure development plans including the 15-year long integrated perspective plan. The committee will work for the development of Indian defence industry and technology advancements.

Organisation

Four sub-committees on: policy and strategy, plans and capability development, defence diplomacy and defence manufacturing ecosystem come under the DPC; the terms of reference and membership of the sub-committees are finalised separately. Specific issues are managed by the committee through its sub-committees.

DPC is chaired by the National Security Adviser, with the service chiefs, defence, expenditure and foreign secretaries being its members and the IDS chief being its member-secretary. The Integrated Defence Staff headquarters in New Delhi serves as the secretariat for the committee. The DPC submit its reports to the *Raksha Mantri* (Minister of Defence).

Chapter 7

Conclusion

In one of the Annual National Congress Assembly before Independence, Hon. Jawaharlal Nehru gave a detailed speech on how the country's economic conditions in the fields of agriculture, industries, defence and the infrastructure should be developed. He had studied in details the processes of economic development under the capitalist/ democratic system and the socio-economic system of Soviet Russia and China and other Communist countries. He was very much impressed by the planning system by Soviet Russia and other communist countries in achieving economic growth of their countries in the field of agriculture and heavy industries. He suggested strongly that economic planning should be adopted for dramatic growth of the country. Large scale industrial production and agriculture growth was the need of hour after Indian political Independent.

There were other views of developing economics. For example, Congress Leaders like Mahatma Gandhi were the staunch supporter of the developing economic growth through small scale industries like Japanese model. But the disadvantage of this method was that the goods produced by the small scale industries were inferior quality compared to the consumer and capital goods produced by the most sophisticated and advanced machines and advanced markets in the world has great demand for such goods.

In Soviet Union and other communist countries, however, the planning was not perfect from the beginning. It had tried the plan improvement through trial and error methods.

In 1921, Lenin introduced the new economic policy of planning economy and First Five Year Plan was introduced during 1928-32. It called for immense investments in heavy industries, steel output was to be more than doubled by 1932. Amid great confusion, the planning mechanism was overhauled, and gradually a 'Command Economy" was established.

Communist method of planning after the mid-1950s entered a state of flux, and highly centralised administrative type of planning inherited after World War II from the Soviet Union by nearly all communist states underwent considerable modifications In Yugoslavia, planners followed the policies very different from those of Soviet model, and the differences also emerged in the practice of other eastern European countries. In the Soviet Union itself, a debate concerning the most appropriate means for implementing plans went on for some years, but, despite numerous efforts on the part of the government to reorganise the machinery of planning, the fundamental drawbacks of Central Planning were never overcome.

In the Soviet Union, subordinate units of the economy (industrial enterprises) operated in accordance with administrative instructions. They did not decide their output or input management decision by negotiation with other enterprises, but were determined by the planners. The state effective criterion of management decision became conformity to plan i.e. to the instruction issued by the Central Administrative planning organs political authorities achieved a high degree of control over resource allocation and were able to enforce their priorities. When the First Five Year Plan ran into trouble, the Government was able to insist on the fulfilment of most of the plans for Key1 sectors of heavy industries, at the cost of drastic fall in availability of consumer goods. At the apex of the system stood the leaders of the communist party, who decided the policy objectives.

It will be seen from above that Soviet Planning was defective in setting priorities. These were decided by the supreme leaders of communist party who were not aware of the needs of the soviet people. As a result, sometimes heavy industries produce the capital goods but no consumers' goods which were in short supply. There was no equilibrium between priority and they were not realistic.

Another defect of Soviet Planning was that review of the implementation plan was not done realistically. Lower managers who were given this job were afraid of the supreme power and in order to please them they used to give report of 100% success of Plan implementation. Soviet leaders ultimately realised the inflected report and were taking plan implementation of 30% lower than reported. But the USA were closely watching the success and were reporting the implementation as fulfilled upto 45%-50%.

In India, we removed these errors/omission in plan preparation and implementation. Planning Commission was set up in India where the Prime Minister was the Chairman of the Planning Commission accompanied by Deputy Chairman and Economic Experts such as Statistician and former Reserve Bank of India Mr. C. D. Deshmukh. These members, Chairman and Deputy Chairman were well aware of the needs of the Indian population as well as the practical persons. First Five Year Plan was implemented in 1951-56. Agriculture was given priority and Industrial growth was given the second priority. The Plan was carefully designed and care was taken to allocate resources on realistic basis. Monsoon was good during the First Plan and plan achieved its target for 4.1% growth by actual growth of 4.5%. The Second Five Year Plan had given priority to growth of heavy industries which was well implemented and the target was achieved. Second Plan was for ₹ 4800 crores while First Plan was for ₹ 2398 crores. There was Deficit Financing and External debt issues in Second Plan. Since massive economic growth was targeted, immense foreign exchange and domestic investments were necessary. India, however, planned external debts well managed in spite of scarce resources by borrowing, bail out packages etc. and IMF and World Bank assisted India in achieving economic growth. Plan expenditure increased heavily in 7th, 8th and 9th Five Year Plans and reached ranging from ₹ 859000 crores to ₹ 929000 crores during this period. External debt burden was entirely taken by the Government of India and these heavy industries were incorporated 100% fully owned by the Government of India. The Plan review for implementation was very effective and realistic.

Government of India incorporated heavy industries from 1953 to 1980 in large numbers. Foreign loans taken were well spread over different years and targets were well achieved.

Since 1991, India started Liberal economic process and share of the Public Sector companies were sold in Bombay Exchange Markets and the Government retained 60% of the share capital while 40% was sold to the Indian public, foreign companies and private and public

Indian companies which resulted in reducing external debt servicing burden of India from 34% to 4% per annual which is well manageable.

Heavy industries like Steel Plants, Oil and Coal refineries, exploration of oil in Bombay High was extracted along with other places which resulted in increasing oil and coal production. Fossil electricity power increased and India now became self-sufficient in agriculture, electricity, fuel, steel, aluminum and other minerals. IIT institutions were set up in Mumbai, Delhi, Calcutta and Madras. Steel industries were established in Bokaro. Industries like HAL were established for manufacturing radar, missiles, defence helicopters, nuclear weapons such as Brahmas anti-missile etc. India was once large leading importer but now it has become the exporter of defence weapons and is negotiating with Philippines for Brahmas missile import to that country.

Indian heavy industries are classified into the Maharatna, Navratna, and Miniratna with following definition. Maharatna is one giving three years with an average annual net profit of ₹ 2500 crores. Average net worth of ₹ 10000 crores for three years or average turnover of ₹ 20000 crores for 3 years. Or ₹ 10000-5000 crore or free to decide on investments upto 15% of their net worth in a project.

Navratna is one which has a score of 60 (out of 100) based on six parameters which include net profit, net worth, total manpower cost, total cost of production, cost of services PBDI (Profit before depreciation, interest and taxes.) and Company must first be Miniratna and have four independent Directors on its Board of Directors before it can be made Navratna.

Miniratna Category I: Must have made the profit continuously for three years or earned net profit of ₹ 30 crores or more in the one of three years.

Miniratna Category II: Have made profit continuously for the last three years and should have a positive net worth.

Following is the list of Public Sector companies set up by the Government of India during five years plans:

1. National Thermal Power Corporation
2. Oil & Natural Gas Corporation
3. Steel Authority of India

4. Bharat Electricals Ltd.
5. Indian Oil Corporation
6. Hindustan Petroleum Corporation Ltd.
7. Coal India Ltd.
8. NTPC
9. Industrial Finance Corporation

It appears that from being Navratna Companies, these companies laid a very important role in developing infrastructure of India and raising production of coal, oil, fuel, defence production, TV, water and electricity (by establishing dams etc.) It would appear that Congress Government has made tremendous progress in setting up these industries and benefits we have been enjoying from these industries after starting full production by these companies. I am very much impressed by their performance. Hon. Prime Minister Mr. Naredra Mody and his BJP Party claim that he had made progress which Congress government has not made in last 67 years is not true.

After Independence, India has made tremendous economic and financial progress in agriculture and Indian agriculture has been now producing 277 metric tons of foodgrains in 2019 from 80 metric tons in 1965 and has become a net exporter of foodgrains from its previously status as large importer of PL-480 importer of USA red wheats!

India has made large progress in infrastructure and has made tremendous progress in improving roads and highways, in progressing railways communication and goods rail transport from Mumbai and other centres to interim places in India. Its local railway passengers' traffic is one of the wonder in India. We are progressing in this field and Bullet train will be started soon from Mumbai to Ahmedabad and then will be advanced to other remote places. In water, War Ships have been constructed and we have made lot of improvement in defence under water.

In air, we have constructed new airports for transport and air traffic has been increased so much that it is competing the rail passengers' traffic. Our air defence has also improved and we have defence planes like Rafael in our defence plane storage. We are also negotiating with Russia to import 5 S-400 war planes to protect us against our neighbour enemies like China and Pakistan.

It is argued that India made no progress in deference preparation during Congress government. This is not true. Congress Government established Bharat Electronics Ltd.; in 1954 for manufacturing defence equipments like Aviation, radars and other advanced defence weapons.

Hindustan Aeronautics was founded in 1940 for manufacturing defence equipments and it makes advanced defence weapons for defending country.

Only no highest priority was given to defence due to higher priority to other sectors which were essential that time. This resulted in China's war with India where huge casualty was suffered on Indian side and Tibet was grabbed by Chinese forcibly. But after that we made good progress in defence and won war with Pakistan in 1965 and 1971. Recently conflict between India and China is going on LAC near Ladach but looking at our tremendous military strength, China is not openly attacking Indian side and in this conflict, India has proved that its military strength is able to compete with China and India can defeat China in war now.

Honourable Modi Government has made good military strength with spending more than ₹ 1 lakh crores on defence budget for the last 5 years. But it is possible because the Country has made tremendous progress in other sectors of the economy. So credit goes to then Congress Government.

Credit goes to then Congress Govt. Modi Govt. has made tremendous progress in Social Welfare Schemes such as Farmers Sanman Yojana under which farmers are given Rs.6 k per year and unorganized workers get monthly pension. country has planned to become self sufficient under "make in India" policy and the Defence preparations are very strong and adequate.Separate planning for budget fo defence has been made and special attention has been paid to military preparation by appointing Defence Planning Commission. We spent Rs. one trillion for our Defence preparation annually.

References used in this book

Wukie- Pedia on the following:

1. Information on First Five Year Plan from 1951-56 to date.
2. Information in details of growth of agriculture in India on development of agriculture under Five Year Plan period.
3. Information in details on heavy industries incorporated as Fully Public Sector Undertakings by Government of India and their success as Navratna companies during Five Year period commencing from 1951 to date.
4. Introduction in details of transportation and infrastructure development under the Five Year Plan period
5. Information in details of performance in Security and defence development in India from 1951-56 to date.

Index

C

D

E

F

G

H

M

N

O

P

R

S

T

U

V

W

Y